PATRICIA A. TAYLOR

A FIRESIDE BOOK
PUBLISHED BY SIMON & SCHUSTER
NEW YORK LONDON TORONTO SYDNEY TOKYO SINGAPORE

EASY
PERENNIALS
CARE

FIRESIDE
Rockefeller Center
1230 Avenue of the Americas
New York, New York 10020

FIRESIDE and colophon are registered
trademarks of Simon & Schuster Inc.

Designed by Bonni Leon

Photos by Patricia A. Taylor
Manufactured in the United States of America

10 9 8 7 6 5 4 3 2 1
10 9 8   (pbk.)

Library of Congress Cataloging in Publication Data

Taylor, Patricia A.
   Easy care perennials.
   "A Fireside book."
   1. Perennials.   I. Title.
SB434.T394 1989   635.9'32   88-30990
ISBN 0-671-67330-3
ISBN 0-671-67283-5 (pbk.)

CONTENTS

EASY
PERENNIALS
CARE

WELCOME TO PERENNIAL GARDENING

O N E

It's easy to see why flower gardening is one of the most popular leisure-time pursuits in our country. It requires both knowledge and creativity or, put another way, intellect and passion. In return, it provides beauty, a sense of accomplishment, and increased appreciation for the diversity and wonder of life on our planet.

Growing perennials should be the perfect way to have a flower garden. Supposedly, you plant a perennial just once and it then proceeds to rebloom in your garden year after year. Alas, this is not always so. Some "perennials" are so temperamental that they die out within a few months if not properly treated. Other flowers are perennial only within limited climate areas of the country. And still other plants need an extraordinary amount of care in order to look good. Gardening with perennials can mean a lot of work.

Fortunately there are a good many easy care perennials, and that's what this book is all about. It is written for people who want the simple joys of gardening without the complicated challenges. It's sort of like starting with dessert first. While there are some truly wonderful plants described in the following pages, there are also many others that you might want to consider for your flower beds once you have become comfortable with gardening (or, as others might plausibly say, once you have become addicted to its pleasures and frustrations).

Using only the easy care perennials presented in this book, you will be able to design an attractive garden that requires little upkeep. Even more important, you will be able to have an *interesting* garden, a living tapestry that will change shape and form throughout the growing season. The title of the book explains it all: with just the minimum amount of effort on your part, you can have flowers blooming in your garden year after year.

PURE AND IMPURE DEFINITIONS OF PERENNIALS

Gardeners do not always agree on what flowers should be called perennials. To some, a perennial is a plant whose leaves and stems die during winter but whose roots send forth new shoots in the spring. This kind of plant is often described in books and catalogues as an herbaceous perennial. Under this "pure" definition, a daffodil is not a perennial because its leaves come from bulbs.

To others, a perennial is simply a plant that keeps coming back year after year. That's the broad definition of a perennial flower used in *Easy Care Perennials*. Thus, you will find descriptions of herbaceous perennials as well as of bulbs and flowers that reseed themselves.

Perennial flower definitions are further complicated by terms such as "half-hardy" or "short-lived." Broadly speaking, these mean that the plants in question do not spend many years in your garden. It takes time and effort to replace plants. In keeping with the theme of easy care, all the plants named in this book will reappear for at least *three consecutive years* in your garden. Thus, gorgeous hybrid tulips which bloom for maybe two years at most are not included in this list, though they are easy to grow in every other aspect.

THE TRUTH BEHIND THE TERM "EASY CARE"

What do I mean by "easy care"? In most cases, the plants described in this book can be placed in any kind of soil where weeds or grasses are now growing. They can resist most diseases and insect pests with aplomb, and need little upkeep beyond occasional watering (and many on the list even withstand drought). All can be grown in at least four-fifths of the United States as well as the coastal areas of Canada.

In a sense, however, one can be a victim of the success of these perennials. Given rich, loose soil, good fertility, and tender loving care, many of these plants go berserk and spread all over the place. For the most part, these are flowers for people who do not want to spend time preparing the garden soil by digging, adding peat moss and organic matter, and fertilizing.

When reviewing the plants described in this book with various mail-order nurseries, I was pleased to hear one person spontaneously comment, "But they are all so easy." That is the intent, and it was nice to hear it confirmed.

HOW THE PLANTS WERE CHOSEN

This is a very personal book in that all flowers are grown in my garden in Princeton, New Jersey. I started with the premise that if a flower could survive in my garden it could survive just about anywhere. I sometimes feel that my flower beds serve as breeding grounds for insects, viral diseases, and strange fungi rather than for plants. These nuisances do rather well because I neither use poison sprays nor spend enough time keeping the garden tidy.

Most of the plants in this book have survived in other gardens as well. Some came to me as clumps dug from the gardens of friends and neighbors. These flower beds were located throughout the country, including Albuquerque, New Mexico; Barrington, Rhode Island; Dodge City, Kansas; Hartford, Connecticut; Lexington, Massachusetts; and Staten Island, New York. The perennials from these gardens all survived long trips by car or plane before being settled here in Princeton. Other flowers described in this book have been obtained from mail-order nurseries and were originally grown in such disparate places as Wisconsin, Ohio, and North Carolina.

In addition, I checked on the suitability of each plant in a wide range of sources, including books and magazine articles. To the best of my knowledge, all plants in this book flourish in gardens across the country.

There is one possible problem area in which I have no experience, and that is animals. I am not bothered by deer or groundhogs. While we have lots of squirrels and an occasional rabbit family that likes to set up shop, our dog, Fergus, has managed to chase away such pests. Fergus, incidentally, is a border collie and intelligent enough to have been trained to stay out of the garden borders. If wild animals are a problem in your area, it might be best to check with neighbors who garden to see which plants will be left unmolested.

All flowers in this book have survived in my garden, growing without the help of fertilizers or pesticides. Here, columbines, coral bells, and Spanish squill put on a great spring show.

HOW THE NAMES WERE CHOSEN

The attempt to name and identify plants has bedeviled gardeners and botanists alike for centuries. Each region or area developed its own nomenclature for different plants. Some of these names are wonders of creativity and imagination. Foxglove, according to garden writer Laura Martin, has over sixty known common names, including fairy's cap, our lady's gloves, and fairy's petticoats.

As Europe emerged from the Middle Ages, however, and communications between the various states increased, it became important for herbalists and physicians to precisely identify medicinal plants, a difficult task when each flower or herb had several different names. This need was further heightened with the discovery of the New World and the wealth of plants that were sent back to Europe.

From these events, the science of botany began to evolve. It needed a universally accepted language and, thanks in large part to the Swede Carl von Linné, that language became Latin.

At the time—the mid-seventeenth century—Latin was the obvious choice. It was the general-purpose language of Europe, used in academic, diplomatic, ecclesiastical, and legal affairs. As William Stern notes in his book, *Botanical Latin*, it was the language of educated men. The herbalists who were starting to record their observations about plants wrote in Latin, Stern says, "because they wrote in Latin about almost everything else."

Carl von Linné did more than write in Latin, however. He sat down and came up with a system for classifying plants. That system was incorporated in each plant's name. It brought order to a chaotic condition and earned von Linné a place in history as the father of modern systematic botany.

But does the name von Linné mean anything to you? Probably not, even if you are a student of garden history. For von Linné not only chose the Latin language to identify plants but he also used it to identify himself, and he is best known as Carolus Linnaeus. This penchant for "Latinizing" names ultimately led to the creation of a new language, called Botanical Latin.

What's fine and good for botanists, however, is a pain for a beginning gardener. It is so much easier to remember—and pronounce—the name purple coneflower rather than *Echinacea purpurea*. This book opts for the easy way and uses a common English name, rather than the botanical name, in the text.

Each plant, however, is initially identified by its botanical name. This is done for two reasons: (1) so that you will be able to identify it correctly when buying it—(five plants, for example, are called dusty miller); and (2) so that you can find it in the many catalogues and books that list plants by their botanical names.

THE FIVE-LETTER GARDENING WORD

Money. No one ever mentions it. Perhaps this is because gardening has long been the province of the rich and well-to-do. Once you start to grow flowers, however, you will find all too quickly that it can be an expensive pursuit.

There are ways to minimize costs. It may be hard to believe, but just by heeding the tips, you could save a considerable sum of money.

1   Get to know other gardeners. Most are pleased to share perennials that have spread beyond their assigned places. As mentioned earlier, many of the flowers I grow have been gifts from other gardens.

2   Stay away from pesticides. These are expensive to buy and time-consuming to administer. The plants named in this book can pretty much survive on their own. There is only one pesticide recommended for use. It's an organic one called rotenone, and you would probably need no more than one or two containers per summer for the plants mentioned in this book.

3   Don't worry about fertilizers. These cost money also, and you will find that most of the plants in this book do quite well without additional plant food. Indeed, my garden is over ten years old and looking better with each passing year. I have never added an all-purpose fertilizer.

4   Use grass clippings as a mulch. These form a blanket to cover bare spaces and smother most weeds. As the grass decomposes it adds nutrients and organic matter to the soil, which is another reason why you don't need to buy fertilizers. You can buy mulches—many of them better looking—at garden centers, but grass is certainly the cheapest. If you don't have enough clippings from your lawn, ask neighbors if you can have theirs.

5   Try growing plants from seed. Many of the plants in this book seed themselves, which is an excellent example of how easy it is to grow them from seed. A packet of seed usually costs about one-tenth the price of a six-pack of perennials. The text descriptions indicate what flowers are easiest to grow from seed.

6   Do some comparison shopping. If you plan on buying a lot of plants to get your garden underway, it would be wise to check on prices charged by various sources. In general, the mail-order nurseries of Bluestone Perennials and J. W. Jung Seed Company offer the least expensive prices for plants described in this book.

THE SIX-LETTER GARDENING WORD

Design. Think about the definition of that word. Whether you examine it as a verb or a noun, it involves work and does not connote a relaxed activity or result. Too often, I feel, design intrudes itself into the pleasure of gardening. True, there are height, foliage, and color factors that you combine to produce an effect; but these need not be taken too seriously. The premise of this book is that gardening is a pleasurable activity, not one that puts you on your best behavior.

To be perfectly honest about it, my garden is nice but not spectacular. Experienced gardeners who come to my garden to be inspired after reading an article I have written invariably say, in the most disappointed tone: *"Oh."* It is so mortifying.

I keep thinking I will do better next year, and over time I have. When we moved to our home over a decade ago, there was nothing but weeds on our small (60 by 125-foot) plot of land. Now when people who don't know I write about gardens come over, they often say, "What a lovely garden," and they mean it. Of course, I love them for it. But even in those wonderful moments, I know in my heart that my garden would still never win an award. I simply do not have the time to make sure that a color scheme is working out or to worry over whether a certain plant will bloom at the right time.

My garden, however, is one that has flowers blooming from late February to early November. The sight of this ever-changing, colorful artwork fills me with pleasure and satisfaction. That's important to remember. While it is great fun to show off your garden, it is in the final analysis a work of art that you have created for your own pleasure.

While I appreciate and enjoy a well-designed garden, I do not have the time or patience to execute one. My garden rambles, as many of its perennials seed themselves or wander at will. The result is somewhat untidy but also quite colorfull.

The picture here, taken in mid-June, features the bright yellows of the sun drops and the lovely white of the feverfew. Just three weeks earlier, this scene was crammed with the pinks and blues of columbines and Spanish squill. This constant, yet colorful, change is one of the joys of perennial gardening.

Hidden underneath this mass of foliage, shoots of perennial ageratum are fighting their way to the surface and, in front of the fence to the left, clumps of boltonia are emerging. In the fall, this garden picture will have evolved to one where blue and white predominate.

HOW THIS BOOK SAVES YOU WORK

In today's busy world, few people can spend hours in the garden. It's an activity to be squeezed in on weekends, with maybe an additional ten to fifteen minutes devoted to watering or cutting flowers on warm weekday evenings. As the popular saying goes, however, haste makes waste. There are several crucial but time-consuming factors that must be considered before you even step into the garden. This book has done most of that work for you.

1   You do not have to look up the temperature zone for each plant. This is provided with every description. In addition, as shown in the map, all but three plants described in this book will grow in gardens in at least 90 percent of the United States; four-fifths of these perennials will grow in every location except those situated along the gulf coast and the beach areas of southern California.

2   You do not have to spend time finding sources for the plants. Mail-order and, where applicable, seed sources are listed for every plant. Some of these are difficult to find; all the tracking work has been done for you.

3   You don't have to acquire a lot of information about growing techniques. For the most part, these plants can simply be plunked in the ground and left to go their own way. Where needed, growing information is included in the text descriptions.

4   You don't have to learn a lot of plant names. This is not an encyclopedia of plants. The book is written on the premise that many people like to start slow when it comes to dealing with plants. Remembering the names of flowers is somewhat akin to walking into a party of strangers and being expected to call them by name after the first introduction. There are only fifty plants described in this book, and that is more than enough to get you started.

5   You don't have to agonize over choices. At first glance this may not seem like a benefit, but it is. There are, after all, over 10,000 daffodils blooming in gardens around the world. Of those thousands, which one daffodil would be a reliable performer for you? Flipping through catalogues filled with luscious colored pictures of hundreds of different kinds, it's hard to know where to begin. This book names names; it presents a specific plant and tells you why it is a good choice.

6   You don't have to worry about season of bloom. The flowers have already been grouped, under separate chapters, in this way for you.

7   You do know that these plants are all easy care flowers. As discussed earlier in this chapter, you do not have to spend time preparing the soil, spraying with pesticides, or replanting.

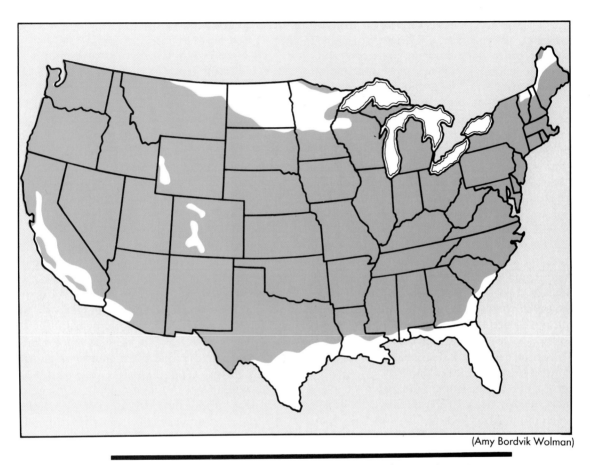

(Amy Bordvik Wolman)

Plants described in this book thrive throughout the United States. Over 90 percent can be grown in the green area indicated on this map; a good 80 percent will grow in every location except the lush warm areas of the Gulf Coast and southern California. When in doubt as to whether or not an easy care perennial is suitable for your area, give it a try—these are all very adaptable flowers.

BUT YOU'RE NOT OFF SCOT-FREE: SITE, SOIL, AND SUN CONSIDERATIONS

When all is said and done, a garden still remains a personal statement. A book such as this one can do some of the work for you, but in the final analysis you are the creator and the designer. There is work for you to do.

Your first task is to choose your garden site. It is advisable to start small, get comfortable with a limited number of plants, and then go on to bigger and better things. There is no best site, just an area where you would want to see some colorful flowers in an attractive planting.

The second step is to take a close look at the soil. As mentioned earlier, if there are weeds or grass growing in your proposed garden area, the soil should be suitable for the easy care perennials described in this book. The weeds, however, will have to go. They need to be completely cleared before you start planting, or they will slowly reclaim their territory.

Suppose, however, that weeds are not a factor; that you are contemplating growing flowers in a rubble-strewn lot or a bare patch of dirt in a new development. In these cases, it is best to have the soil checked out. That's easily done: just scoop up several samples, put them in plastic lunch bags, and go to your nearest garden center or county extension service agent and ask how you can find out if the dirt is suitable for growing grass or weeds. Remember, you don't want the rich, fertile soil most people associate with flower gardens, because the majority of these perennials will spread too fast in such a setting.

Drainage is a dull but necessary subject that has to be considered in discussing soil. Check your proposed garden area after a heavy rain. If there's long-lasting puddles of water, you have a situation in which most plants drown. You have two options: (1) improve the soil so that it drains better—and that generally means digging down a good two feet, mixing in sand and peat moss, and then refilling the spot; or (2) pick another site. It's a lot easier—and cheaper—to do the latter.

Your third, and last, initial consideration is to check carefully on the amount of sunlight the proposed site receives—and not only on one particular day but also at various times of the year. A patch that receives full sun in early spring, for example, could be in deep shade when the leaves unfold on a nearby tree.

As far as plants in this book are concerned, you can count on all of them growing in partial shade; that is, a spot during the day when they receive some sun and then bright shade for the remainder of the time. If you have a potential garden spot that receives full sun or that spends most of the day in shade, check the charts in Chapter Six. These list, by season of bloom, the easy care perennials most appropriate for different light situations. In addition, the individual flower descriptions often include information on light requirements other than partial shade.

HOW TO USE THIS BOOK

Once you've chosen your garden site, checked its soil, and noted the amount of sunlight it receives, it's time to start browsing through the rest of this book. The next four chapters are grouped by season of bloom, an important consideration in planning a garden. Height is also a crucial factor but one that cannot be pinpointed precisely. Because a plant's height is often dependent on other growing conditions—particularly sun and soil—it is often difficult to give an exact measurement. You will find height guidelines under each plant description as well as reasons why these might vary in different garden settings.

You will see a temperature range in which each plant can be comfortably grown. When in doubt as to whether a perennial will survive in your area of the country, give it a try—these are all tough plants. Each plant description also includes the names of companies selling the plant. The addresses and phone numbers of these firms, as well as a brief review of each, are presented in the appendix.

If you feel you still need a little more help after you've chosen the kinds of plants you want to grow, turn to Chapter Six. There you will find some information on how to plan and start a perennial garden. Design considerations, such as color combinations and themes, are also reviewed under the discussions of the different kinds of gardens.

Have fun reading about these wonderful flowers. It's hard to go wrong with any of them. All will add color and interest to your garden and provide you with great pleasure for many years.

EARLY
SPRING

TWO

It is so joyous to see green shoots and then colorful flowers emerge from the brown earth of early spring. On an April day in Princeton, you can see the pink blossoms of bishop's hat and bleeding heart, the blue flowers of the Jacob's ladder, and the white and pale yellow of the "Ice Follies" daffodil.

Early spring is probably the most joyful time of year to garden. Even if the winter months have not been harsh, they have been dark. Now the days are getting longer and there is an unmistakable feel of mildness and new life in the breezes.

A garden bed seems to be a mystery that can no longer contain itself. Everywhere there are signs of green growth and awakening. The earth soaks up the warmth of the mellow spring sun and appears to be melting (and literally is, in areas where frost has gripped it).

It's a bright time of year. Daylight cascades about, spilling through trees and shrubs that have yet to form thick canopies of green leaves. Areas that will be flooded with shade in just a few months are now basking in sunshine. These are all good sites for early spring bulbs—especially the snowdrops, which start to bloom in late February in Princeton.

It's a wonderful time to be outside, and somehow it seems a privilege to do the necessary chores. These include raking leaves, which gives you a chance to see all the new growth emerging underneath, cleaning out leftover weeds such as dandelions, and peeling up any moss, which is easily done at this time of year.

Once the garden looks neat and rather bare, take a good, hard look at it. Try to visualize what it was like last year. Are there any changes you would like to make? Any new plants you would like to add? Then, when winter weather briefly returns with a last blast of cold wind or wet rain, cuddle up inside with a garden book or mail-order catalogue and review possible additions to your flower beds.

BISHOP'S

EPIMEDIUM GRANDIFLORUM

HAT

For areas where winter lows are within the range of −30° to +20° F.

PLANT SOURCE: Carroll Gardens

Foliage shapes and forms provide an underlying elegance to all gardens. Thus, it seems rather fitting that the first plant described in this book is one grown chiefly for its handsome green leaves. Bishop's hat is a hard-to-find treasure that is best suited for adding a touch of class to quiet nooks and crannies.

When daytime temperatures begin to reach 50° in early spring, small green shoots of this plant start emerging. Soon there are many thin, wiry stems about 12 inches tall. In two or three weeks, the stems boast small, green leaves and lovely, pink-and-white flowers.

The flowers last for about three weeks and then disappear. The attractiveness of this plant continues, however, for the leaves grow and fill out, eventually forming an elegant clump.

My bishop's hat came to me from the garden of Corinne Rowley in West Hartford, Connecticut. There, it grew in rich, moist soil by a tree.

Though I did put my plant in the partial shade that it prefers, my soil had been a weed patch for years and is quite dry in summer. Thus, my bishop's hat is not as tall or as lush as that growing in the Rowley garden; indeed, its foliage has a thirsty look in the heat of summer.

After two or three years in my garden, the bishop's hat began to develop a rust in late July or early August. Rusts are fungal diseases that live up to their names by sprouting rustlike growths on a plant. These growths eventually turn the leaves so brown and brittle that they fall off. None of the literature that I have searched refers to this disease striking bishop's hat. Nevertheless, there it is in my garden. I solve the problem by simply snipping away the dead foliage.

This might seem like a negative recommendation but in fact it is not. Even with its shorter height and midseason rash, the bishop's hat is an easy care member of the garden. Aside from cutting the flowers in spring and pruning the sick foliage in summer, I have done nothing with this plant since bringing it back from West Hartford over ten years ago. It is so wonderful in spring—the first true herbaceous perennial to make its appearance—and so refined that I would be loath to lose it.

As mentioned in the beginning, this is a very difficult plant to find. There are two reasons for its shortage in the trade. It does not spread rapidly; thus it takes several years for a nursery to grow enough stock to offer it for sale. White Flower Farm, for example, has sold all its offerings of bishop's hat and is currently growing more plants for sale in 1990. Also, as soon as it is put on the market, it quickly sells out. One nursery owner reported that it is not unusual to have people with large estates call up and order all available plants.

While bishop's hat is best suited for a shade or woodland garden, it will even look good in full sun, as long as the soil is rich and well watered. If you have a chance to obtain this almost secret garden treasure, grab it.

BLEEDING

DICENTRA EXIMIA

HEART

For areas where winter lows are within the range of −30° to +30° F.

PLANT SOURCES: Busse Gardens, Carroll Gardens, Native Gardens, Piccadilly Farm, Primrose Path, Sunlight Gardens, White Flower Farm

SEED SOURCE: Thompson & Morgan

When I first started my garden over ten years ago, I was desperate for plants that would spread rapidly, look lovely, and not make any time demands. My mother-in-law, who was weeding wild bleeding heart out of her garden, took the pointed hint and gave me a clump. She did warn, however, that I might regret the gift. I never have.

This bleeding heart has been placed in various beds around my home. In late April and throughout May, it bears pink, teardroplike flowers on 12- to 18-inch stems. I have learned that in dry, claylike soil with full sun, it produces few flowers and does not spread at all. In a moister setting, with loamier soil and partial shade, it both blooms profusely and multiplies rapidly. That has not been a problem for me because clumps are easily pulled out and used in cut-flower arrangements or as gifts.

The wild bleeding heart literally pales in comparison with the larger Chinese or old-fashioned bleeding heart, *Dicentra spectabilis*. The flowers on this bleeding heart are much more colorful and striking. This handsome plant has a serious drawback, which has kept it out of my garden: the foliage disappears after it flowers and the garden is left with an empty spot for most of the growing season.

The foliage on *Dicentra eximia*, the wild or fringed bleeding heart, blooms all growing season and is silvery green in color and fernlike in appearance. I would recommend the plant for its foliage alone. It looks great in cut-flower arrangements and pretty in the flower bed, especially one that is in semi-shade and consists of the quiet colors that go particularly well with silver-green.

One summer we had a particularly wet August, and I was surprised to see the plant blooming again, although not as profusely as it always does in early spring. Since that discovery, I always give the wild bleeding hearts an extra good soaking when I water the garden. They reward me for this treatment with sporadic bloom until the first frost.

Wild bleeding heart spreads through seeding. According to Andrea Sessions at Sunlight Gardens, ants help this process by carrying the seeds about and then dropping them. That's all that's necessary—how easy to grow can a plant be? If you don't have a friend who wants to give you excess bleeding heart plants, growing them from seed would be the next cheapest way to introduce this perennial to your garden.

BUGLOSS

BRUNNERA MACROPHYLLA

For areas where winter lows are within the range of −30° to +20° F.

PLANT SOURCES: Burpee, Busse Gardens, Carroll Gardens, Crownsville Nursery, Holbrook Farm, Lamb Nurseries, Milaeger's Gardens, Sunlight Gardens, Wayside, White Flower Farm

This rather unusual plant was discovered in the Caucasian Mountains about 150 years ago. In the spring, it bears beautiful, warm blue flowers that look like a swarm of forget-me-nots hovering over the plant. After these delightful flowers fade, the leaves continue to grow, eventually forming a large clump that rivals the hosta plants in size and shape. The leaves are dark green, rough in texture, and resemble huge hearts. They are quite elegant in the garden border.

Bugloss is supposed to propagate itself readily by seedlings. In the ten years that I have grown it, I have had only one plant pop up unexpectedly. Mine does grow in the semi-shade that is best for this plant but it is never watered, and I suspect this lack hinders further bugloss plants from appearing. If you want to try growing bugloss in full sun or almost complete shade, do— but be sure to water it frequently.

Fortunately for me, the bugloss clumps do get larger over time and are easily divided. I have dug up small shoots in early spring and put these in other garden areas with no problems at all.

This is a plant that is often described as pest free. Something in my garden, however, likes it. My chief suspect is the slug because there appear to be slug slime trails along many of the nipped leaves. In addition, my plant has some kind of viral disease that makes itself known by leaving black spots on the leaves. If I cut the infected leaves off and remember to water the plant periodically, the infection appears to go dormant. In spite of these afflictions, my bugloss manages to hold its own. It always looks wonderful in the spring and fairly respectable throughout the rest of the growing season.

One aspect about this plant that I really like is that there are no cultivars and no other species grown in the garden. Perhaps it is so perfect that no one has bothered to try and improve upon it. The only confusing element is that it was once classified as *Anchusa myosotidiflora*, and some catalogues—most notably Carroll Gardens and White Flower Farm—insist on retaining this inaccurate identification.

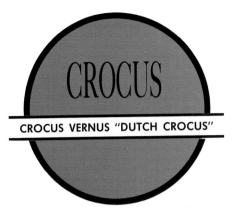

CROCUS

CROCUS VERNUS "DUTCH CROCUS"

For areas where winter lows are within the range of −20° to +30° F.

CORM SOURCES: Burpee, McClure & Zimmerman, Wayside

Crocuses are known to have brightened people's lives with their cheery colors and undemanding natures for over 3,000 years. While there are about eighty species, the one most often found in gardens today is a descendant of the large, tough common crocus *(C. vernus)*. Dutch breeders have been working with this crocus for the past 200 years and have developed many different hybrids. These are known as Dutch crocuses; the original *Crocus vernus* has just about disappeared from public view and is not offered by any major nursery.

Dutch crocuses are distinguished by their large size—anywhere from 2- to 4-inch flowers. Totally hardy, their cells are unaffected by recurrent freezing and thawing. Indeed, many other crocus species cannot survive the cold winters that these crocuses can.

The common crocus self-seeded prolifically, and occasionally the Dutch crocuses will revert back to type and do the same. The purple crocuses in my garden do this. If I wanted to, I could dig up the self-sown crocuses, making sure the green leaves were not harmed, and plant them in places where I think they should be. Generally, however, I let them roam.

Every planting guide on crocuses will tell you that they need to be planted 3 inches deep in the fall. This always puzzled me because I could not figure out how a seed produced by a crocus in my garden could burrow that deep and form a corm for the next year. I finally solved my mystery and it's an interesting story.

A corm is different from a bulb. It is a fat, underground stem covered with fibrous leaf bases. Temperature change triggers a reaction, and the food stored in the swollen stem is used as an energy source for producing roots and leaves and, finally, the flower. The new green leaves then start the process all over again by storing up energy to create a new corm on top of the old. That's why it is so important to let crocus leaves wither away naturally.

As the new corm is built, it forms what is known as contractile roots. These literally pull the corm down to the right depth in the soil so that it can bloom the following year. How's that for letting a plant do all the work for you? When you plant the corms in the fall, however, it's a little late in the year for the roots to do their job; that's why you have to dig down 3 inches.

Squirrels have a particular fondness for these flowers. If you watch the animals closely, you can catch them nibbling away, with purple crocus leaves dripping from their mouths. While there's no denying the annoyance of such a sight, there's not much you can do about it. Try planting extra crocuses on the supposition that after the feasting is over, there will still be enough left for your viewing pleasure.

DAFFODIL
NARCISSUS 'ICE FOLLIES'

For areas where winter lows are within the range of −25° to +25° F.

BULB SOURCES: Burpee, J. W. Jung, McClure & Zimmerman, Wayside, White Flower Farm

It appears that the debate over whether these lovely spring flowers should be called daffodils or narcissus is at least 300 years old. In 1646, the English botanist John Parkinson complained how idle and ignorant gardeners referred to some daffodils as narcissus. "All know that know any Latine," he wrote, "that Narcissus is the Latine name, and Daffodill the English of one and the same thing."

Actually Parkinson did not know his Latin as well as he thought he did. According to the *Oxford Dictionary of English Etymology, daffodil* also derives from a Latin word. Over time, however, the more Latin sounding *narcissus* became accepted as being more proper and is now recognized as the true botanical name for the genus.

So, where does all this leave the person who likes to know the real names of flowers in the garden? First, you can't go wrong with narcissus. It is the botanical genus for all these plants. Second, call it daffodil if you like and don't worry about it. Purists might want to know that

the yellow, trumpet kinds of these flowers—the ones with long snouts—are referred to as daffodils in horticultural circles.

If you think the name of this flower is confusing, trying to pick out just the right one for your garden is even worse. Daffodil bulbs hybridize freely in nature and, in the hands of horticulturists, amateur gardeners, and professional nurserymen, this has been taken to extremes. It is estimated that in the past 150 years, approximately 10,000 varieties of daffodils have been created.

In an effort to make some order out of this gorgeous mass, the 1955 Horticultural Congress appointed the Royal Horticulture Society of London to come up with a classification system. The society created a series of divisions based on flower proportions. Thus, some catalogues will refer to trumpet daffodils or double daffodils or flatcup narcissus. These are all based on the system set up by the society.

There really is no one best daffodil for a garden. It all depends on what color, height, and bloom period you want. If you are looking for a steady, reliable performer, however, it's almost impossible to go wrong with 'Ice Follies.' Wayside Gardens calls it "one of the finest daffodils in existence." White Flower Farm describes it as one of their favorites.

'Ice Follies' is a flatcup from Division 2; it has one large flower, with the cup or trumpet section shorter than the flanking petals. It is a sturdy plant, with strong stems and an ability to handle early spring weather.

In addition to its durability and reliability, this daffodil gives you the best of color combinations: it starts off with white petals and a yellow center and then, as it ages, gradually turns all white.

GRAPE
MUSCARI BOTRYOIDES
HYACINTH

For areas where winter lows are within the range of −35° to +25° F.

BULB SOURCES: Burpee, McClure & Zimmerman

This odd little flower—a tall, skinny, triangular cone covered with tiny blue balls—has been grown in gardens for at least 400 years. Its first written record appears in the catalogue of John Gerard, an English surgeon and gardener who in 1596 published a record of the 1,100 varieties of plants in his London garden. The grape hyacinth had already traveled a good distance to reach Gerard's garden, because the plant's original home is in southern Europe and the Caucasus.

The flower pictured here is known as the common grape hyacinth and is one of a group of about forty species. Some of its cousins have more exotic flowers or more yellow in their blue. You can see their pictures in many nursery catalogues. All are quite easy to grow and are supposed to self-seed and thus naturalize freely.

My grape hyacinth came to me as a gift, and if it had been an "uncommon" kind, I probably would have been just as happy. But I like the thought of growing this particular one, of knowing that it has brightened gardens for centuries and that it is sturdy enough to have lasted all these years. That's the kind of tough-minded plant I prefer for my garden.

Further proof of its durability was provided in a September 1986 *New York Times* article by

Grape hyacinth shoots pop up in early fall . . .

Jeanne Carens. Ms. Carens gardens on the shores of Long Island Sound and grows plants that need to survive high winds, salt spray, near tide flooding, and hurricanes. This was the only shallow-planted bulb that managed to survive under such conditions.

All grape hyacinths, however, do have the very disconcerting habit of arriving too early at the party; that is, they send up green, onionlike shoots in the fall that look rather ugly. It's the grape hyacinth's way of letting you know that come spring the *bona fide* flower will make its appearance in that spot. There's absolutely nothing that you can do about these shoots; they are a necessary part of the plant's growth pattern.

. . . but the flowers do not appear until early spring.

JACOB'S
POLEMONIUM REPTANS
LADDER

For areas where winter lows are within the range of −35° to +15° F.

PLANT SOURCES: Carroll Gardens, Crownsville Nursery, Primrose Path, Sunlight Gardens

It may be hard to believe that this elegant and refined plant is actually a wildflower. Nevertheless, it can be found growing in woods and bottomlands from New Hampshire to Georgia all the way west to Minnesota and Oklahoma. These locations tell you something about the plant's preferences: cool, moist sites in partially shaded areas. The plant will grow in full sun as long as the location is not too hot nor too dry.

The popular name, Jacob's ladder, comes from its foliage. Horizontal pairs of leaflets march up the stem, and these are supposed to match the ladder that Jacob dreamed of in the Old Testament. Unfortunately, there is a close cousin with similar foliage and it has the same popular name. This is an excellent example of why it is so important to know the botanical name in order to get the correct plant.

Polemonium reptans, the Jacob's ladder discussed here, blooms in early spring. Its stems are between 8 and 15 inches tall and are covered with delicate blue flowers. These are long lasting in cut-flower arrangements; as the blossoms age, they turn white. *Polemonium caeruleum*, the other Jacob's ladder, blooms in late spring and early summer and has taller stems.

For some reason, *Polemonium reptans* has fallen out of fashion. It is a fine, old garden plant, "one well worth universal cultivation," as Alice Morse Earle wrote in 1901.

I like it not only for its early bloom and elegant appearance but also for its nice-looking foliage throughout the rest of the growing season and for its totally undemanding nature. The four nurseries listed on this page also agree with this assessment and offer it. In addition, Wayside Gardens and White Flower Farm also feel it is a plant that merits more attention. Because sales are so low, however, they do not list it in their catalogue every year. Both should be offering it by 1990.

Clumps of Jacob's ladder should be divided every three or four years. In addition, the plant seeds itself and you will often find baby clumps growing near a large one.

In the heat of high summer, spider mites may start sucking the foliage of this plant. The mites are hard to spot, but their devestation is not: tiny brown pinpricks in the leaves. If this happens in your garden, just give the Jacob's ladder extra water until cool weather arrives.

SIBERIAN

SCILLA SIBERICA

SQUILL

For areas where winter lows are within the range of −40° to +30° F.

BULB SOURCES: Burpee, McClure & Zimmerman

The rich blue flowers of the Siberian squill are among the earliest of the garden year. Both the popular and the botanical name of this plant reflect its origin in Siberia, where it was discovered about 150 years ago.

The very name Siberia conjures up images of harsh conditions and survival of the fittest. Hav-ing been born and raised in such a tough envi-ronment, this early spring charmer seems impervious to pests or diseases. Because of this, gardeners around the world have planted its bulbs and enjoyed its beauty.

A British garden writer at the beginning of this century noted that Siberian squill "thrives on the mountains of North Italy, where masses of it may be seen growing close to the snow and in this country it withstands the wind and rain which would be the ruin of many other flow-ers."

At the same time, the American writer Alice Morse Earle was commenting on what a favorite this flower was and how it grew in her mother's garden. Louise Shelton, a garden writer from Morristown, New Jersey, noted in her 1912 book that the Siberian squill always bloomed in March.

Dependable performer that it is, this little flower still blooms every March in New Jersey. Its blue petals burst forth right after the white ones of the snowdrops. If weather conditions are just right, the two will often bloom together —making a striking combination on the dull brown winter earth.

Each little Siberian squill plant consists of several 6-inch stalks, with three to four gor-geous blue flowers per stalk. The flowers hold up well when cut, lasting almost a week. Left on their own in the garden, the flowers often go to seed and you will find the plants spreading throughout your flower beds.

The folks at McClure & Zimmerman, who obviously want to sell lots of these bulbs, claim that an ambitious gardener can plant 200 of these in an early fall hour. Not being the ambi-tious sort myself, I simply transplanted some from a neighbor's garden in May. I tucked the bulbs about 3 inches into the ground and let the foliage ripen naturally. There are many cultivars offered; I am perfectly satisfied with the species plant.

SNOWDROPS

GALANTHUS NIVALIS

For areas where winter lows are within the range of −30° to +30° F.

BULB SOURCES: Burpee, J. W. Jung, McClure & Zimmerman, Wayside

British garden writer Lys de Bray has uncovered a wonderful story about how this lovely little plant came into being. According to her research, medieval lore told of snow falling when Adam and Eve were expelled from Eden. The two were so miserable with the cold and wet that an angel took pity on them and touched the falling snowflakes. These were instantly turned to snowdrops, the herald of spring.

Snowdrops have provided welcome cheer to many cultures throughout history. During the Middle Ages, for example, they were grown in monastery gardens and were put on church altars for the Feast of the Purification of the Virgin, in early February.

In Princeton, snowdrops usually bloom the end of February and provide just the encouragement one needs at that bleak time of year that winter will not go on forever. Because the temperature is so cold, the flowers last a long time —almost a month in my garden.

Given their popular name and time of bloom, it is not too surprising to learn that snowdrops are among the hardiest flowers known to gardeners. *Galanthus nivalis* is the most dependable of all and the best for naturalizing. It grows 4 to 6 inches tall and holds its own against freezing temperatures, late snows, and strong winds.

If you would like these wonderful little flowers, just plant them any time after spring bloom through early fall, about 3 inches in the ground. They will spread in two ways: through self-seeding and through producing new bulbs.

If you want, thin the clumps to increase the spread. An American garden writer, Laura Martin, suggests that you can take a clump of such thinnings and let them bloom indoors. Once their flowers have faded, you can then transplant the bulbs back to your garden. If you don't want to do this work, that's fine—the snowdrops will do quite well on their own.

VIRGINIA
MERTENSIA VIRGINICA
BLUEBELL

For areas where winter lows are within the range of −30° to +25° F.

PLANT SOURCES: Burpee, Busse Gardens, Carroll Gardens, J. W. Jung, Milaeger's Gardens, Sunlight Gardens, Wayside, White Flower Farm

SEED SOURCE: Thompson & Morgan

An American wildflower, the Virginia bluebell was classified over 200 years ago by a German and named in honor of F. C. Mertens, a professor of botany at Bremen. It is a very lovely, unassuming plant, one that can be found growing unattended in moist, shady spots from New York to Alabama and west to Kansas.

It appears to have made its way into cultivated gardens soon after its discovery. Alice Morse Earle, writing in 1901, noted that the Virginia bluebell was already classified as an old-fashioned flower. When she was a young girl, she recalled, "they were called blue and pink ladies when we hung them on pins for a fairy dance."

The Virginia bluebell is also one of the few American flowers to find favor in the gardens at Windsor Castle. Lanning Jones, columnist for *The London Sunday Times*, described them in one of his books as follows: "The Virginia bluebell has colonized in drifts through the shrubberies to the south of the peat walls. Its clusters of pinkish buds and pale blue flowers are so beautiful that a visit should be arranged to the gardens when they are at their height."

While I have yet to find any printed mention of pests or disease bothering the Virginia bluebell, something affected the plant on the right. The plant on the left—only 3 inches away—thrived. Gardening can be very mysterious at times.

As indicated in these two descriptions, the flowers on this plant change color as they mature. At first their buds have pink tones, but as they open they gradually turn pale blue. The flowers are borne on stems 1 to 2 feet high and look quite elegant next to bright yellow or white daffodils.

Supposedly, there are no pests or diseases that bother this plant. As shown in the picture, however, one plant in my garden was quite sick and the other very healthy. Why this is so, I do not know. If you find a Virginia bluebell that does not perform up to par, simply transfer it to another spot in your garden and see if it likes its new location better. Virginia bluebell does best in cool, moist soil in a shady area.

Most books advise against transplanting this flower in spring and say that fall is the best time to do so. This presents a problem because the plant disappears—goes dormant in horticultural terms—by late June and leaves no trace of its existence. My original plants came from a neighbor's garden; I just dug them up and replanted them in spring. If you want to do it right, mark where the bluebell grows when it has finished flowering and then transplant the roots you find in that spot the following fall.

LATE
SPRING

THREE

You will have cool, refined colors in your garden
with the flowers described in this chapter. As shown
in the arrangement, candytuft, columbine, phlox,
and Spanish squill are all in bloom at the same time.
The gray foliage of the silver king adds an interesting
accent now and throughout the garden year.

Late spring—the period from May through mid-June—is one of the most rewarding seasons of the garden year. Flowers are blooming everywhere, their scent filling the pleasant evening air. Periodic spring rains take care of most watering chores. And while insects and weeds are hatching and germinating, they do so discreetly and have yet to make their presence felt.

For some, it is a busy time of year with many a balmy afternoon spent planting seedlings bought at local garden centers or through the mail. For others, it's a time to relax outside on a picnic blanket or a deck chair and to savor the unfolding beauty all around.

Unless plant markers have been placed to indicate where flowers are located, many an emerging green clump presents a mystery. Is it a friend or foe? In all cases, it's best to wait and give the plant a chance to prove itself. Sometimes it's an unexpected gift from a seed dropped by a passing bird or borne through the wind. Other times the clump eventually reveals itself as a weed that should be pulled out. In many cases, however, especially where the clump is particularly big and strategically situated, it's a perennial whose existence had been forgotten. In this last instance, it's always a pleasure to welcome a plant back.

And there are many greetings at this time of year. One-third of the flowers reviewed in this book make their appearance in late spring. Only one—the Spanish squill—disappears after blooming. The rest stay on, some to bloom for several more weeks and others to serve as handsome foliage plants. The latter provide a cool green contrast in form and size to the bright summer flowers to come.

BELLFLOWER

CAMPANULA PERSICIFOLIA

For areas where winter lows are within the range of −30° to +30° F.

PLANT SOURCES: Bluestone Perennials, Carroll Gardens, Crownsville Nursery, Holbrook Farm, Milaeger's Gardens, Primrose Path, White Flower Farm

SEED SOURCE: Thompson & Morgan

This tall, lovely blue flower has been in gardens for generations. It is a member of a large genus with about 300 species. These family members come in a variety of sizes, shapes, and living styles. Some bellflowers, for example, are short annuals found in formal garden beds while others are 6-foot perennials happy in the wild.

This particular bellflower has an aura of mystery about it. It was given to me by Lisa Corey, a friend who lives in Lexington, Massachusetts. She had raised it from seed and placed it in her most impressive looking garden—a 50-foot flower bed backed by an old New England stone wall.

During a July visit to her home, I watched Lisa cut the 3-foot stalk to the ground, dig out a small clump of roots and the nest of green leaves that crowned them, and then hand the whole thing to me in a small plastic pot. She assured me that the plant would not only survive in our car for the next week of my family's

travels but would also do well in my garden. Lisa was right.

I planted the bellflower in a partially shaded spot and then forget about it—so much so that I nearly pulled it out as a weed the following spring. (The moral to this incident—and it is an important digression—is that you should *always* mark where you put your plants.)

Through sheer happenstance, I placed this flower next to a clump of silver king. The bellflower bloomed the following June and the two perennials looked terrific together with the silver foliage of the one providing a cool backdrop for the blue flowers of the other.

The mystery surfaced when I wrote to Lisa and asked her for the precise botanical name so that I could properly identify the plant for this book. Lisa replied that it was *Campanula persicifolia "Telham Beauty,"* which is the name of the plant offered by White Flower Farm and the seeds offered by Thompson & Morgan. The folks at Carroll Gardens, however, believe that this identification is probably incorrect because, as a cultivar, *"Telham Beauty"* does not produce seed. Carroll Gardens sells a plant identified as *Campanula persicifolia caerulea*, and its description fits that of the plant in my garden. Bluestone Perennials also uses this name. Other nurseries listed on this page opt out of the debate by listing just *Campanula persicifolia* or by selling different cultivars of this plant.

All of which makes one wish that people would stop producing and touting so many hybrids and cultivars. It's too confusing for a beginning gardener and even for many a knowledgeable one. If you see the description "peach-leaved bellflower" or some variation similar to that, the flower is similar to the one in my garden.

In any case, all agree that *Campanula persicifolia* in any form is a wonderful plant: long lasting and attractive in the garden, durable, just about immune to diseases and pests, and easily grown in sun or semi-shade. It increases in two ways: through root spread and by self-seeding. That last fact indicates how easy it is to grow from seed. Budget-conscious gardeners might want to try this approach rather than buy plants.

CANDYTUFT

IBERIS SEMPERVIRENS

For areas where winter lows are within the range of −30° to +30° F.

PLANT SOURCES: Burpee, Carroll Gardens, Milaeger's Gardens, Primrose Path

SEED SOURCES: Harris Seeds, Park Seed

Candytuft is an old-fashioned plant that is a must for every garden. It is slow to spread, dependable, and maintenance free. And there's more. It's good looking throughout the year with evergreen stems resembling thick pine needles, and it becomes truly spectacular when crowned with its white blossoms in May. Supposedly, if you cut these flowers before they go to seed the plant will bloom again. But I have tried this several times and it has never worked for me.

Candytuft is a southern European plant that first came to England in 1731, where it was an instant hit. It was brought to our country by colonists and became a garden staple during the nineteenth century. Then and now, its 6- to 9-inch height makes candytuft a perfect plant for the front of the garden.

This is a plant that can be grown in every state. Nothing—not even slugs—bothers it in my garden and it spreads at a very leisurely pace. When I feel it has outgrown its assigned area, I dig up the excess and plant it elsewhere.

Until the hot, dry summer of 1988, the transplants always settled comfortably into their new homes. That summer, however, two candytuft colonies almost succumbed to the heat while the old, established planting appeared unaffected. When fall came, both transplants perked up. Thus, if you are introducing candytuft to your garden, don't despair if it has some initial difficulties in establishing itself.

Candytuft can be grown in full sun or partial shade. I have noticed that the more sun it receives, the more white flowers it produces in May and June. The blooms are not longlasting in cut-flower arrangements but do fine in the short term, such as in a centerpiece at a dinner party.

There are many cultivars of this plant, each with its own particular merit. They come with names such as 'Purity,' 'Pygmae,' and 'Autumn Snow.' If you want to try these do, but note that they usually cost more than the species plant.

CHIVES

ALLIUM SCHOENOPRASUM

For areas where winter lows are within the range of −35° to +25° F.

PLANT SOURCES: Bluestone Perennials, Burpee, Carroll Gardens, Crownsville Nursery, Milaeger's Gardens, Native Gardens, Primrose Path, White Flower Farm

SEED SOURCES: Burpee, Harris Seeds, Park Seed, Thompson & Morgan

Too often, when people think of chives they envision green snippets decorating a salad or crowning the sour cream on top of a baked potato. While there's no denying the refreshing taste of this mild member of the onion family, too many people relegate it to the vegetable patch or herb garden and fail to recognize it as an attractive plant for the flower bed.

In late spring you will find it covered with delicate, lilac-colored blossoms on 10-inch stems. These are pretty, long-lasting additions to cut-flower arrangements. If you let these flowers stay in the garden they will produce seeds, and other chive plants are likely to make an appearance over time.

For all practical purposes, these plants are disease and pest free. There are no special growing requirements. They will perk up a garden in full sun or partial shade, in rich or poor soil. With sun and good loamy soil, however, they will produce bigger clumps and spread more easily.

One nice thing about chives is that the more you cut them, the more they seem to grow. If they receive lots of water, they will continue to bear flowers through summer and fall. Even without abundant watering, they will still bear

the green stalks used for seasoning. When winter comes, the plant goes into hiding and there is nothing for you to clean up.

Chive seedlings are a popular mail-order item (usually found under listings for herbs) and can be bought at most local garden stores as well. The least expensive, albeit slower, way to introduce chives to your garden is to plant a row of seeds. Remember, this plant can seed itself; it shouldn't be hard for you to grow it from seed. Buy a seed packet from a local nursery or any popular seed catalogue and follow the directions. You will soon have an attractive, trouble-free, and tasty plant in your flower garden.

COLUMBINE
AQUILEGIA VULGARIS

For areas where winter lows are within the range of −30° to +30° F.

PLANT SOURCES: Crownsville Nursery, Primrose Path

SEED SOURCE: Thompson & Morgan

The columbine shown here is quite different from the American one usually pictured in books and catalogues. This is the European columbine, a hardy plant often called granny bonnets because of its appearance. The flower spurs are short and curve inward, forming in shape the top part of a hat, while the flaring petals compose the brim. In the more familiar American columbine *(Aquilegia caerulea)*, the spurs are long and graceful and seem to float behind the flower petals.

Now that the European columbine is established in my garden it would be extremely difficult for me to grow the American one; the two cross-fertilize with abandon and the new flowers almost invariably resemble the European parent. If you want the American columbine, be sure to fence out all the Europeans from your garden borders.

In describing the European columbine, the British writer Lys de Bray noted that, "this is a plant that is often inherited with an old garden and it is impossible to get rid of the myriad seedlings that spring up year after year." That's why I like this flower; it just fills my garden with all different shades of blue, purple, and pink summer after summer. Sometimes the plants are a solid color—a rich, deep, dark purple is particularly gorgeous—and sometimes they are a combination of white and another hue.

I like the randomness of the plant and never know from year to year what colors will predominate. One year there were ten different shades of pink; in others, purples or dark blues have dominated. All appear on stems ranging from 1½ to 2½ feet in height and grow in part shade or full sun.

Once the flowers have finished blooming—and there are so many that I cut them freely for indoor arrangements and still have hundreds outside—I let them go to seed. The petals will fall off, and inside the remaining part of the flower tiny black seeds will grow.

When I can see the seeds inside, I cut the stalk and then shake it over all parts of the garden. That's how I plant next year's crop. It takes no more than ten minutes to do this each year. New seedlings will spring up in a month

or so—depending on the amount of rain the garden gets—and these will produce the next year's flowers. How's that for being an easy care perennial?

Columbine has one very bothersome pest, known as leaf miner. This little insect literally mines a leaf, digging its way through and leaving a trail. Since columbine is so prolific at producing new seedlings, and since the insects appear to attack the older plants first, I just cut off the infected leaves, put them in a plastic lawn bag, and quickly dispose of them so that the infestation can be curtailed. This simple method does away with the unsightliness of the pest and allows the seedlings enough growth to be adorned with exotic flowers the following year.

CORAL

HEUCHERA SANGUINEA

BELLS

For areas where winter lows are within the range of −30° to +30° F.

PLANT SOURCES: Busse Gardens, J. W. Jung, Milaeger's Gardens, Piccadilly Farm, Primrose Path, White Flower Farm

Coral bells are relative newcomers to the garden scene, having been discovered in southwestern U.S. just about 100 years ago. They became favorites very quickly, both here and in England. The following points explain why.

1   Coral bells are very neat, self-contained plants. They form clumps generally no more than 1 foot in diameter and do not sprawl or become messy.

2   The coral bell leaves are exceptionally good looking and tidy (neatness counts, even in the garden) and some garden designers favor it for this factor alone, using the plants as an edging in the flower border.

3   In May, each coral bell plant will begin to send up 12- to 18-inch-tall stems crowned with dainty flowers that look like tiny bells. These add an ethereal touch to the garden scene, hovering above the plants like a swarm of color.

4   The tiny blossoms, adorning the long, slim stems, look great in flower arrangements.

5   There is a long bloom period—up to two months if spent stalks are cut and the plant is well watered.

6   In most areas of the country, the leaves stay evergreen, providing garden interest during the bleak winter months.

7   Coral bells require little care. If frost heaves them out of the ground, all you have to do is put your hand on the plants and firmly press them back in. To transplant, just break off a root with some leaves on it and stick this in the ground.

Garden writers differ on the best growing conditions for this plant. Some say full sun is best, others that it needs semi-shade. My coral bells grow in semi-shade and do fine. Plants in the garden of my neighbor Jean Woodward do even better. Jean's grow in full sun and seem to stand taller and bloom longer. Since my plants are descendents of hers, I think the extra sun has something to do with their better appearance. Garden books also warn that mealy bugs and root weevils can be a problem; fortunately, they have not been in my garden.

Breeders have been busy with this plant and have come up with a number of different cultivars. Some are white, others pink or red; some are shorter, others taller. I believe mine are species plants. Their ancestors were growing in Jean's garden when she and her husband moved to our street over forty years ago. These coral bells are hardy, tough, and reliable—just the way species and easy care perennials should be.

FERNS

ONOCLEA SENSIBILIS

For areas where winter lows are within the range of −30° to +30° F.

PLANT SOURCES: Busse Gardens, Carroll Gardens, Primrose Path, White Flower Farm

Ferns are survivors. They have endured the Ice Ages and have been eaten by the dinosaurs. For almost 400 million years, they have grown, evolved, and adapted to our planet. When you look at a fern in your garden, you are looking at our prehistoric heritage.

Botanists estimate that there are about 10,000 species of ferns in existence today. Some—such as the tree ferns of Chile, New Zealand, and South Africa—are gigantic plants up to thirty feet in height. Others are small, delicate creations. Ferns have accommodated themselves to a wide range of growing conditions and can be found on all continents, including Antarctica.

Nevertheless, despite the ancient heritage and broad geographic dispersion of ferns, individual species are quite fussy and precise. They have evolved to grow in specific habitats, and if a setting is altered drastically, the fern ceases to exist. That's why it is difficult to transplant a fern from a wild, wooded area to a domesticated garden area. As far as the majority of ferns are concerned, there is no place like home.

The fern pictured here, popularly known as the sensitive fern, is a nice exception to this situation. It can grow in full sun or shade, from the plains of Canada to the marshes of Florida. How then did such a tough plant get the common name sensitive? The answer lies in its reaction to frost: just one cold contact and the fronds shrivel up and disappear until the following spring. As if to compensate for such a drastic reaction, however, the sensitive fern leaves behind 12- to 18-inch stalks with spore-bearing pods. These are sometimes known as "bead sticks" and look great in dried flower arrangements or in the winter landscape.

While this fern is not as elegant as the cinnamon or maidenhair fern, it does offer ease of care, good foliage contrast, and handsome contributions to dried flower arrangements. It also spreads quite rapidly—some even say it is invasive. You need only buy one or two sensitive ferns to begin, and in a few years you will have more than enough.

FOXGLOVE

DIGITALIS PURPUREA

For areas where winter lows are within the range of −25° to +25° F.

PLANT SOURCES: Burpee, Carroll Gardens

SEED SOURCES: Park Seed, Thompson & Morgan

There is something medieval about the spires of foxgloves in the spring garden. From 4 to 5 feet tall, their lavishly flowered stems tower over other plants and resemble the elegantly carved crowns on gothic cathedrals.

Foxgloves were blooming when those churches were built and have continued to give visual pleasure down through the centuries. In Cornwall, England, for example, they burst forth each spring from the tall hedgerows that loom over country roads, creating a splendid flower border without any human assistance.

Given their beauty and ease of care, it is not surprising that they were among the first plants brought to the New World by colonists. Foxgloves adapted well to our country and have now naturalized themselves in northern California, Oregon, and Washington. Summers are relatively cool in these areas and the foxgloves thrive in full sun. In hot, dry areas such as our Midwest, however, foxgloves tend to wilt and are best grown in partial shade with frequent watering. They grow in partial shade in my garden and are simply splendid plants.

Most sources attribute the common name, foxglove, to folk myths. Supposedly, bad fairies created the flowers as gloves for the paws of foxes, enabling these creatures to sneak up quietly on their prey. The botanical name, *Digitalis*, comes from the Latin for "finger" and reflects this story.

Foxglove has a long history of medicinal use. In medieval times, extracts from the plant were used to "cure" a variety of diseases ranging from catarrh to ulcers. In the late eighteenth century, however, foxglove became respectable in medical circles. A doctor in Shropshire, England, had noticed that people with heart problems seemed to be helped by the herbalists using foxglove concoctions. His research led to the discovery of digitalis, of which foxglove is the primary source. Indeed, the drug is named for this plant.

Left to its own devices, the wild foxglove will come up in a variety of colors, ranging from white to purple. The darker the color, the more digitalis the plant contains. Some gardeners do not like the random-color nature of this plant and suggest that if you want one color only—say, white—you must snip off all other-colored flowers before they have a chance to set seed.

Strictly speaking, foxgloves are biennials; that is, a seedling will appear one year and the flowers the next. They seed themselves so readily, however, that it really doesn't matter what they are just as long as they keep coming back every year.

Your best and most inexpensive bet with this flower is to buy a packet or two of seed. Open the packet and follow the planting instructions. Or just sprinkle the seed lightly about your garden in June (just the time when the foxglove flowers would be doing the same thing). Make sure that your garden doesn't suffer from drought during this period, and in two or three weeks you should find foxglove seedlings popping up.

Sometimes, in the heat of high summer, the parent plants will get quite sickly looking. If you don't like their appearance, just cut the stalks to the ground. Toward the end of summer, before the weather gets too cold, transplant the seedlings to where you want flowers the next year. From then on, the foxglove will take care of the seeding program itself, and you will have a wonderful attraction in your garden year after year.

HOSTA
HOSTA UNDULATA

For areas where winter lows are within the range of −30° to +25° F.

PLANT SOURCES: Burpee, Busse Gardens, Carroll Gardens, Crownsville Nursery, J. W. Jung, Lamb Nurseries, Milaeger's Gardens

Hostas are Japan's exquisite gift to the garden world. Europeans discovered these plants growing there almost two centuries ago and were enchanted by their grace, durability, and ease of growth. Hostas were a particular favorite of P. von Siebold, a Dutch nurseryman who was one of the first on the continent to import and breed them. By the late 1800s, von Siebold was responsible for introducing over three dozen kinds of hostas to European gardens—an accomplishment which is acknowledged in the several Siebold cultivars still grown in gardens today.

Hosta has long been called funkia and plantain lily. Though some nursery catalogues still use these descriptions, most now call the plant by its true botanical name of hosta—an identification honoring an Austrian botanist named Host.

In North America, hostas are grown from mid-Alabama north to mid-Canada. In addition to weathering such temperature extremes, this truly versatile plant can be grown in full sun or deep shade. For best results, however, it should be grown in partial or light shade. Hostas need moist soil; they limp along in dry conditions.

With the increased popularity of gardening in recent years, hostas have gained renewed attention from plant breeders. There are now over 400 kinds to choose from and some are truly lovely—and expensive!

The beginning gardener and those on a tight budget are perhaps best advised to start with *Hosta undulata*, often referred to as *Hosta variegata*. This is a real workhorse of the garden—and yet few plants are more striking in the border. Its leaves have undulating margins and are a handsome white and green. In midsummer, there are 3-foot-tall spikes of lilac-colored flowers that look well in cut-flower arrangements. Don't be surprised if the leaves on this plant turn all green by the end of summer; it just happens occasionally and has nothing to do with the plant's location or its health.

There is one pest that could present problems: slugs. These creatures favor the same cool, moist situations that are best for hostas. When you start seeing lots of large, ragged holes in your hostas' leaves, chances are slugs have been feasting on them.

If you're not too particular, you can either let the leaves look ragged or pick off the slugs with your hands. If such actions seem distasteful, you have two other possible approaches: (1) cut off a small clump, including the roots, and transplant it to a spot which slugs have yet to discover or (2) try the chemical slug baits that can be bought in most garden centers.

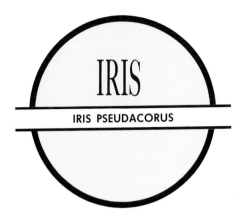

IRIS

IRIS PSEUDACORUS

For areas where winter lows are within the range of −15° to +35° F.

PLANT SOURCE: Busse Gardens

The spring garden comes into full regal splendor when irises bloom. Tall and stately, these aristocratic flowers unfold their lovely plumage day by day. Their colors range over a wide spectrum, with only true red missing.

And yet, in spite of their great beauty and popularity, irises can be difficult flowers to grow. They are often eaten by slugs, attacked by iris borers, and infected with a soft rot that has a dreadful odor. In addition, their foliage flops over in a state of dishabille after a spring rain and is not particularly attractive once the flowers have faded. In summary, most irises are not candidates for an easy care garden.

There is an exception, however, and it is a wonderful plant called the yellow flag. This is a great-granddaddy of the iris breed, having been in gardens for centuries. Many believe it is the inspiration for the *fleur-de-lis* depicted in heraldry. The English essayist John Ruskin gave a true description when he wrote that it is a plant "with a sword for its leaf and a Lily for its heart."

Given its popular name, the yellow flag does bear a strikingly attractive yellow flower. It is a short bloomer, however, and quickly fades. The true distinguishing feature about this iris is its foliage. Many grow it for this reason alone. The 3- to 4-foot-tall, curving wands make an elegant addition to any garden. Under ideal conditions —a sunny spot in marshlands—the foliage can reach 6 feet in height.

The yellow flag can be found growing wild in both Europe and North America, particularly along lake borders and other wet places. Several books place this iris in the bog-plant category, yet it is such an accommodating plant that it will grow in drier situations as well. It thrives in sun or bright shade but does not like dark, gloomy places.

Without question, the yellow flag has beauty, grace, and hardiness. It is also unbelievably easy to grow. Just scratch a hole in the soil that is deep and wide enough to cover the rhizome (the iris equivalent of a bulb) and its roots. Plunk these in, cover with the dirt, and pat down firmly. That's it.

If your area happens to be particularly dry, it would probably be a good idea to water frequently. Otherwise, leave the plant alone and let it grace your garden year after year. It will spread slowly in two ways: through forming new rhizomes and through self-seeding. Ambitious gardeners can cut the stalks to the ground in the fall; neat gardeners will clear away the dried, dead leaves in early spring when sprucing up the garden; and lazy gardeners will let nature perform its own clean-up work in due time. Remember, this is a plant that grows wild. There is no right approach; just whatever suits each individual gardener.

Yellow flag is frequently mentioned as being totally free of problems. This is not quite true. As mentioned several times in this book, I rarely use pesticides and do not spend a lot of time checking on the health of plants. Under these conditions, my yellow flags have occasionally suffered from borers, rots, slugs, and black vine weevils. Amazingly, these plants have survived and even increased. They are beautiful with their graceful foliage arching over clumps of green and white hosta leaves while flanked by the contrasting but equally tough fronds of the sensitive fern.

If you want elegance and ease of care in your garden, you'll have both when you plant the yellow flag iris.

For areas where winter lows are within the range of −25° to +25° F.

PLANT SOURCES: Bluestone Perennials, Busse Gardens, Crownsville Nursery, Milaeger's Gardens, Native Gardens, Primrose Path, White Flower Farm

SEED SOURCES: Harris Seeds, Thompson & Morgan

When Gertrude Jekyll, England's grand turn-of-the-century garden designer, planned a flower bed, she invariably included lamb's ears and it's easy to see why. The gray, woolly foliage is elegant along a border and provides a soothing contrast to and transition between colors and foliage.

When Tim Steinhoff, a Brooklyn landscape designer, was asked in 1987 to create a garden for the southwest corner of 14th Street and Union Square, in New York City, he also chose lamb's ears. And, once again, it's easy to see why. This plant not only looks good but is also tough enough to withstand the pollution and abuse that all city plants have to endure.

About the only thing that lamb's ears does not like is prolonged hot, humid weather. "They

Many gardeners regard these as insignificant and pinch back the stems to prevent the flowers from appearing. Others, however, think the flowers are attractive. To each his or her own. Flower arrangers, however, do value these flowers because they are everlasting.

Though lamb's ears is a member of the mint family, it does not spread as fast as many of its relatives. After three years' growth, however, it is not unusual to see a dead spot in the center of the clump. This is a signal that it's time to divide the plants—a task that can be carried out anytime during the growing season. You can plant the offshoots in sun or semi-shade and, like their parents, find that nothing will bother them.

About the only trouble you will have with lamb's ears is locating it by its botanical name. *Hortus Third*, the source used for this book, says the correct botanical name is *Stachys byzantina*. Many nurseries list it as *S. lanata* instead; others choose *S. olympica*.

This is a classic example of the current disarray with regard to plant names. Supposedly, the botanical names were created to end the confusion arising from multiple folk names. And now we see three botanical names being bandied about for lamb's ears.

Help and, it is hoped, clarity are in the making. The American Association of Nurserymen is currently working with the U.S. National Arboretum to compile a standardized list of botanical and common plant names. The schedule calls for having agreed-upon names for 9,000 plants by 1992. In addition, a seven-digit computer code has been created to identify plants. This code incorporates each plant's botanical name and will eventually be used in all publications describing plant performance.

It's a mammoth project but when it's completed, life will certainly be a lot simpler for garden writers—and for those trying to locate lamb's ears by its botanical name.

tend to melt in our Georgia summers," Carleen Jones of Piccadilly Farms explains. The Jones family has found a cool spot in their garden where the lamb's ears will grow but they have discontinued mail-order sales because many southerners have had poor results with this plant.

Though grown chiefly for its foliage, lamb's ears does send forth flowers. Opinions are mixed as to their merits. The flowers consist of tiny purple blossoms on thick, gray, woolly-coated stems that get about 18 inches high.

MOUNTAIN

CENTAUREA MONTANA

BLUET

For areas where winter lows are within the range of −30° to +20° F.

PLANT SOURCES: Bluestone Perennials, Carroll Gardens, Lamb Nurseries, Milaeger's Gardens, White Flower Farm

SEED SOURCE: Thompson & Morgan

When we moved to our house on a warm, September day over ten years ago, the "gardens" consisted of a mass of weeds, and not much else. I thought there might be some daffodils in the spring, but such was not the case.

Thus, I cleared the front bed with great vigor and with little thought of damaging anything the following April. While pulling out the awful hydra-rooted mugwort weed, I came across a little group of leaves that somehow had a touch of character about them. They looked too refined to have arrived in the garden by chance. That's when I realized the previous occupants must have once attempted a garden, and that's how I became acquainted with mountain bluet.

I had no idea what it was going to be. I left it alone and watered it periodically. By late May, it had gotten rather bushy and about 2 feet tall. The early grayness of its seedling leaves had given way to a more greenish gray. I noticed flower buds forming, but these looked somewhat like pine cones.

Then, one morning I went out and was greeted with the most wonderful blue flower. It opened its arms to let the light stream through and looked like a lace pattern on top of a stem. At first, I was reluctant to cut any of the flowers. In later years, however, I just had to put them in flower arrangements where they were quite long lasting. This also encouraged further bloom, though in my garden it is rather sporadic. Patricia Leuchtman, a writer who gardens in the Berkshires, reported in a newspaper article that her mountain bluet not only rebloomed but continued to do so after several hard frosts.

This is a plant that has been described as being invasive, yet has increased very slowly in my garden. There are two factors, I believe, that contribute to its restrained growth. The first is lack of full sun, which the plant is supposed to favor. My mountain bluet is located in partial shade and appears to put most of its energy into producing its lovely flowers.

The second is that the foliage on my plants is usually attacked by a rust disease or spider mites—I'm not sure which and have found no reference to such problems in garden literature. This usually happens in late July or early August, and I solve the problem simply by cutting the foliage to the ground. This rather drastic remedy does not deter the plant from blooming for me the following year. Even if more care were required, I would still keep the mountain bluet. As White Flower Farm says, it is a fine garden plant.

PEONY

PAEONIA LACTIFLORA 'FESTIVA MAXIMA'

For areas where winter lows are within the range of −30° to +20° F

PLANT SOURCES: Burpee, Busse Gardens, Carroll Gardens, White Flower Farm

Peonies are regarded as an aristocratic flower in China, where they are known to have graced gardens for at least 2,500 years. About 200 years ago, they were brought to Europe and shortly thereafter crossed the ocean to the gardens of

wealthy Americans. "In old New England towns," Alice Morse Earle wrote in 1901, "fine peony plants in an old garden are a pretty good indication of the residence of New England Brahmins."

Chances are that many of these New England gardens featured "Festiva Maxima." This lovely, fragrant peony was introduced in 1851 and is still, according to White Flower Farm, the standard by which new varieties are judged. Another gardening book has dubbed it one of the greatest white varieties in the world.

This peony is a double—that is, crammed with petals—and inside its mass of white softness one usually sees tiny flecks of red. It grows about 3 feet tall and always blooms in time for the Princeton, New Jersey, Memorial Day Parade.

For all its grace and sweetness of smell, this is one tough peony. It came to me on a September afternoon in the form of bare roots dug up by a friend. She wasn't quite sure how to plant them, so I just put them in the ground at the edge of our vegetable garden in an adjoining field and covered the roots with dirt. The next year, almost all the plants came up.

When we moved to our current home, I left one plant behind. That peony continued to come up year after year, loaded with an ever-increasing number of white blooms. It received no fertilizer, no special watering, no cutting back in the fall, and as an almost further test of strength, soon grew in the midst of thick field grasses.

Luck had something to do with this marvelous record. "Festiva Maxima" peonies need lots of sun, good drainage, and little or no fertilizer; those were the growing conditions in the field.

The plants I moved to my new home have not performed quite as well. My husband and I had followed generally recommended transplanting instructions. We dug up the field peonies in September and cut the roots (technically, the thick fleshy part underground is called a rhizome) so that each had three to five "eyes" (the same way a potato has "eyes"). Then, we put the cutting into a hole about 2 feet across and 18 inches deep, covered it with soil mixed with sand and bonemeal, and made sure the "eyes" were covered with 1½ inches of soil.

After all that work, the flowers were just not up to snuff the following year. At first I decided the plant needed time to settle in. The next year, with bloom only slightly increased, I had to look for another cause. The culprit, I finally decided, was lack of sun. Whereas the peonies would get a full day of sunshine in the field, they were now only getting about six hours.

Though not in the same quantity nor with the vigor of their former home, these peonies continue to put forth lovely fragrant white flowers in May. It's hard to imagine a garden without them, and once you have them in yours, you will readily agree.

PHLOX

PHLOX DIVARICATA

For areas where winter lows are within the range of −30° to +25° F.

PLANT SOURCES: Busse Gardens, Piccadilly Farm, Primrose Path

SEED SOURCE: Thompson & Morgan

Every spring there is a pause in the bright colors that march through my garden: the daffodils have shed their last petals and the candytuft has yet to burst forth. This is a quiet moment, and it is filled with the light, airy blooms of the wild blue phlox.

This is a plant that grows in moist woodlands from Quebec all the way down to northern Alabama. It is often suggested for a wildflower garden, but it really should be considered for an easy care one, too. It was brought back to England in 1739, where it was enthusiastically received and where you can now see it growing in many spring gardens.

There is really nothing that you have to do for this plant—it either makes it or it doesn't. Just place it in a shaded or semi-shaded spot and it will spread through underground roots. The short, ground-level green leaves will send up 12- to 15-inch stems in April, and these will bloom for a good month or more. The flowers are both long lasting in cut-flower arrangements and wonderfully fragrant. They are definitely worth a sniff as you stroll through your garden.

Rabbits are supposed to love this phlox; if there are a lot of these creatures in your area, you might not be able to grow it. It needs a moist soil. This phlox can dry up and literally disappear during rainless summer heat. Don't worry if this happens in your garden. The phlox will come back with the following year's spring rains.

In the summer my phlox is often covered with white blotches, which I assume to be some sort of a fungus. Since the leaves are so low growing and hidden in the middle of the garden, the blotches do not bother me—and do not seem to mortally bother the phlox, either.

SILVER

ARTEMISIA LUDOVICIANA
VAR. ALBULA "SILVER KING"

KING

For areas where winter lows are within the range of −25° to +30° F.

PLANT SOURCES: Bluestone Perennials, Burpee, Carroll Gardens, Crownsville Nursery, Lamb Nurseries, Milaeger's Gardens, Wayside

Silver king adds a designer's touch to the garden. It is grown chiefly for its lovely silver-white leaves, which always look smashing next to green foliage and provide a nice break between clashing colors—say, red bee balm on one side and yellow sundrops on the other. It also adds a cool touch to a more muted combination of blue campanulas and soft pink bleeding hearts.

This plant is just about indestructible—which is why some people call it a weed and why others find it spreads uncontrollably in their gardens. The key to keeping this plant in its place is poor soil, preferably the thick, muddy kind. Silver king will do well in such a home but will not become invasive.

Silver king hails from the American Southwest, where it was discovered almost two centuries ago. It obviously thrives in hot, dry, sunny places. Gardeners soon found that it does fine in cool, partially shaded areas as well. It can now be found in gardens throughout this country and in southern Canada.

Like a teenager, silver king behaves according to its setting. In a moist, partially shady spot it will get 3 feet tall and sprawl. In a dry, sunny location, it will form a gorgeous bushlike clump up to 5 feet in height. When viewing this clump at night, especially when a full moon is out, it is easy to see why silver king has acquired the nickname ghost plant. It shimmers eerily and yet quite splendidly, under such conditions. This setting also gives one greater appreciation for its botanical name, *Artemisia*, which is in honor of Artemis, Greek goddess of the moon.

One added bonus needs to be mentioned. Silver king is great in flower arrangements, both fresh and dried. In fresh arrangements, use it as a foliage accent, much as ferns are used. In dried-flower arrangements, just pick off the flower heads (which look like thin, pebbly versions of the leaves) and place them in the arrangement. There's no special drying requirements; the plant does it all on its own.

The only problem that I have had with silver king is an attack by an insect known as the four-lined plant bug. This little critter chews tiny round holes in the foliage; a sprinkling of rotenone dust solves the problem. I have read that rust diseases can attack the plant; such diseases periodically destroy other flowers in my garden but they have never harmed the silver king.

SPANISH SQUILL

ENDYMION HISPANICUS

WOOD HYACINTH

For areas where winter lows are within the range of −20° to +35° F.

BULB SOURCE: McClure & Zimmerman

This is the scentless, country cousin of the more elegant, fragrant hyacinth. As its popular name indicates, it is native to Spain and can often be found growing wild in spring woods. It is a longtime favorite, having brightened up Elizabethan flower beds as well as those of the early American colonists. Should you ever visit the gardens in the Royal Park at Windsor in late May, you would find masses of these flowers carpeting woodland glades with pink, white, and blue blossoms. Spanish squill is a wonderful plant in any kind of garden, but especially in an easy care one.

Just plant the bulbs in fall, about 2 to 3 inches deep in a soil that is well drained (that means long-lasting puddles do not form after rain). As far as light goes, you will find this flower is most adaptable: it can grow with or without direct sun. If you place it in partial shade, however, it will outdo itself in blooms.

Once you've put the bulbs in your flower bed, you can wipe your hands of any further involvement. In the spring, they will send up green shoots and then 8- to 10-inch-tall stems. These will be loaded with lovely pink, white, or blue

flowers. You can add them to cut-flower arrangements if you like.

By midsummer, the foliage will have disappeared. The plants will have already formed extra bulbs for the next spring and might even have reseeded themselves. If you would like to dig up some of the bulbs for transplanting, this is a good time to do so. This flower has absolutely no watering or fertilizing requirements and is rarely attacked by pests or diseases.

Your major problem in adding Spanish squill to your garden will be locating it in catalogues. It is often described as *Scilla hispanica* or as wood hyacinth. In addition, most mail-order nurseries offer cultivars rather than the species plant. McClure & Zimmerman, however, does offer the species Spanish squill under its correct botanical name.

There is a very similar plant, known as English bluebell *(Endymion nonscriptus* or *Scilla nonscripta)*. While many prefer this version because it is fragrant, it is not as hardy as the Spanish squill.

SPIDERWORT

**TRADESCANTIA X ANDERSONIANA
"BLUE STONE"**

For areas where winter lows are within the range of −20° to +30° F.

PLANT SOURCES: Carroll Gardens, Milaeger's Gardens

Spiderwort was one of the first American plants brought to England. It was discovered in Virginia by, and eventually named for, John Tradescant, gardener to King Charles I. In some ways, it is like a daylily, being covered with blossoms that open one day at a time over several weeks. However, spiderwort is useless as a cut flower and is grown chiefly for its looks.

In its wild habitat—moist, shady areas from Connecticut to Georgia and west to Missouri—these looks were not classified highly by flower fanciers. Indeed, garden writer Alice Morse Earle noted in 1901 that the plant was "so little cared for today that it is almost extinct in our gardens." Then a hybrid, *x. andersoniana*, was developed and caught the fancy of many gardeners. White Flower Farm insists that this hybrid "is a perennial that deserves far more attention."

Once spiderwort arrives in your garden, plan on having it stay for awhile. Whether wild or hybrid, it is a plant that spreads. For this reason, garden writer Allen Lacy periodically curses the plant and rues the day he ever put it in his garden. As with many other plants described in this book, the poorer the soil, the less likely spiderwort will become too rampant.

I like spiderwort for three reasons: (1) It is ridiculously easy to grow in either full sun or partial shade. I just bought some seedlings from White Flower Farm, put them in the garden according to the instructions, and that was it; (2) It has a lovely blue color on its 2-foot-tall stalks. The flowers look especially rich when the yellow sundrops are bursting all around them; and (3) It has a second life. After the first bloom is finished in late June or early July, I cut the stalks to the ground. These obstinate plants proceed to send up new shoots, which bloom throughout the fall, surviving the first few frosts with ease. I usually have blue spiderworts flowering well into November—a time when most gardens are filled with only the yellow and reds of fall.

While I have no complaints about my spiderwort cultivar, White Flower Farm now thinks it is inferior to a new one called "Zwanenburg

Blue" and will no longer offer "Blue Stone." Supposedly, the former has larger flowers that are a clearer blue. If you want to try this new cultivar, do. Personally I see no reason to trade in the "Blue Stone," which continues to be offered by the nurseries listed on page 60.

SUNDROPS
OENOTHERA FRUTICOSA

For areas where winter lows are within the range of −20° to +30° F.

PLANT SOURCES: Bluestone Perennials, Carroll Gardens, J. W. Jung, Native Gardens, Piccadilly Farm, Primrose Path, Sunlight Gardens, White Flower Farm

Sundrops are all-around garden performers. These cheerful, easily grown plants look like ground covers in winter and spring, burst forth with lemon-yellow blossoms for almost the entire month of June, and then have their leaves turn dark red in the fall. They are really just super.

Sundrops operate on a two-tier system. The bottom level consists of dark green rosettes that look like ground covers. These leaves are very shallow rooted and spread rapidly. If you happen to yank a clump out of the ground by mistake, simply press it back in with your hand. The shallowness of the roots is a blessing, for if you find you have too many of these plants, they can easily be pulled out of the garden.

The second tier consists of a 2- to 3-foot-tall stem with dark green leaves and a thick crown of yellow flowers. Much like daylilies, these open one or two at a time, which is one reason why the plant blooms for so long.

I rarely get to see the foliage turn deep red because Japanese beetles emerge almost as soon as the last yellow petal falls, and they begin their annual feast on the stem leaves. The result is a rather ugly mess, and once the beetles have gone, I either cut the stems to the rosettes on the ground or pull out the plants.

Throwing away some of the plants is probably beneficial, since it adds some space to the crowded clumps. The stem-cutting does not deter the rosettes from continuing to spread about through the rest of the summer and from being loaded with bright yellow flowers the following year.

Sundrops have two closely related relatives that bear similar flowers. The cousins that bloom in late afternoon are known as evening primroses. Since the flowers are so alike, the day-blooming sundrops are also often called evening primroses (which goes to show yet again how important it is to know the correct botanical name for a plant).

Another cousin is a midwestern favorite and is known as the Ozark sundrop *(O. missourensis)*. This plant has much larger flowers, sprawls, and is a favorite in rock gardens.

My sundrops will grow in sun or partial shade, and spread about in most any kind of soil. They are truly easy care and add a strong dash of color to the garden. If you like bright yellow, this is a flower for you.

SUMMER

FOUR

Easy care perennials make for a very colorful summer
garden. In this picture, feverfew and rose campion,
two of the earliest flowers brought over by the Puritans,
team up handsomely with two American natives—
coral bells and coreopsis.

Summer is a time to relax and truly enjoy easy care gardening. From late June through August, flower production seems to go into high gear while you sit back and reap the profit. As you will read in the following pages, there are many plants to choose for your viewing pleasure.

While it is convenient and helpful to categorize flowers by season of bloom, don't forget that many follow their own schedules. Plants that start flowering in late spring, for example, and that continue on through early summer include chives, columbine, coral bells, and mountain bluet. These add blue, purple, pink, and lavender hues to your garden while bright yellow sundrops—another spring holdover—welcome the onrushing summer heat.

Foliage plants—such as the silver king, the warm green sensitive fern, and the light-gray, woolly lamb's ears—grow lush and fill in empty garden spaces. This is the time of year when the garden is at its fullest, crammed with colorful growth.

Your chores are few and simple during this hot, lazy season. Sprinkle grass clippings (or, if you like, more expensive but better-looking mulches such as peat moss) around the plants to preserve moisture in the soil and to smother weeds; water when the flowers look droopy; and cut back and discard any diseased or infested plants. That's about it.

Summer is the season when the variety of a perennial garden is perhaps best appreciated. Your flower beds will present one lovely tapestry of color in July and a totally different one in August. This ever-changing aspect is most evident when you leave for a vacation. In just two weeks' time, the garden can change dramatically. Best of all, with the easy care plants described in this chapter, it does so all on its own.

ASTER FIRKARTII

ASTER X FRIKARTII 'WONDER OF STAFFA'

For areas where winter lows are within the range of −10° to +25° F.

PLANT SOURCES; Bluestone Perennials, Burpee, Canyon Creek Nursery, Carroll Gardens, Crownsville Nursery, Lamb Nurseries, Milaeger's Gardens, Wayside, White Flower Farm

When you place aster frikartii in your garden, you are planting a flower with impeccable credentials. Consider the following.

1   A proven performer, it was recognized as a sterling plant almost from the moment it was developed by Herr Frikart of Switzerland three-quarters of a century ago.
2   It received the highest possible rating among perennials evaluated by the University of Georgia for use in the South.
3   English plantsman and noted garden writer Alan Bloom has characterized it as simply "superb."
4   Milaeger's Gardens in Racine, Wisconsin, says that "without doubt it's the longest blooming aster; in fact, few perennials can match it in this respect. This plant is a must for any perennial garden."

Indeed, the only people who could possibly have anything negative to say about this plant would be those who hate the color lavender-blue. In areas with moderate temperatures, such as Princeton, New Jersey, this 2- to 3-foot-tall plant will bloom from late June through September or October. In frost-free climates, it is supposed to be ever-blooming.

Alan Bloom (and what an appropriate last name for a plantsman) says that aster frikartii does not need to be staked if given light and lots of air. Obviously something is amiss in my garden because this aster flops dreadfully if not supported. I think the culprit is lack of full sun; my plants get only five to six hours a day.

If you feel ambitious, you could pinch back the stems—much as one does for chrysanthemums—to encourage more branching and greater flower production. Since aster frikartii is such a consistent heavy bloomer anyway, I have not bothered with this chore.

What I find particularly impressive about this plant is that nothing seems to bother it. While I have read that mildew may be a problem in humid weather, this has not happened to my plants. Some grow near bee balm, and when the leaves of that plant are covered with the white dust of powdery mildew, the aster frikartii continues to bloom on unaffected.

ASTILBE

ASTILBE x ARENDSII

For areas where winter lows are within the range of −20° to +20° F.

PLANT SOURCES: Bluestone Perennials, Carroll Gardens, Crownsville Nursery, J. W. Jung, Lamb Nurseries, Milaeger's Gardens, Wayside, White Flower Farm

SEED SOURCE: Park Seed

These elegant flowers honor Georg Arends, a German plantsman born over a century ago. Arends devoted his life to raising and breeding many different kinds of perennials. He began by developing new hybrids of hostas, phlox, rhododendrons, sedums, and campanulas. Many of his creations among these plants are garden favorites still in use today.

He was aware of astilbes, he later wrote, but thought of them as plants with "rather small, meager spikes." Those in his parent's nursery were mostly an unattractive off-white color.

In 1900, Arends came across a pink astilbe and liked it so much that he decided to cross it with the ones in the nursery. He saw such possibilities in the resulting plants that he went on to breed astilbes for more than thirty years. Thanks to his enormous effort and creativity, we now have truly elegant plants in our gardens.

Astilbes are valued for many reasons. Chief among them is their appearance. Their foliage forms neat clumps of dark green leaves, often

deeply cut. From this green nest, tall spikes of delicate, feathery flowers arise—sometimes as high as 5 feet. The dirty off-white color that Arends began with has disappeared, and in its place is a range from snow white to soft pink to bright red. If you felt so inclined, you could buy a combination of plants that would allow you to have a garden of astilbes in bloom for almost two months.

These plants do not like blazing heat, so they need to be placed in the shade down South. Elsewhere, they can grow in full sun or partial shade. They like water and are one of the few plants in this book that need to be fertilized. My astilbes have been in the garden for five years now, and I have yet to perform this essential chore. For this reason, I am sure, their bloom is not as spectacular as it is reputed to be. I also know I should have divided the plant after three years—and thus increased my supply in the process—but somehow I have not gotten around to that, either. Perhaps this year.

I think it a tribute to Arends that the hybrids he developed have done well in my garden despite my minimal care. I have two highly rated favorites: "Peach Blossom" and "Deutschland." The latter is a bold white and looks great with the yellow sundrops and blue spiderwort. Either of these astilbes are great in an easy care garden. Here, I feel, the choice is one of color and time of bloom. Read the descriptions of the

A. arendsii hybrids in the catalogues published by the nurseries listed on page 69, and then choose astilbes whose height, color, and time of bloom best suit your garden.

While Arends was a superb hybridizer, he was not meticulous about naming his plants. Indeed, he gave the same name—"Deutschland" —to two different cultivars; and the guess is that he felt the second to be superior to the first. Since the first was never pulled from the market, however, both are currently being sold. I have no idea as to whether I have the first or second version. There's even a good possibility that I have neither. Astilbes not only crossbreed freely, they also tend to mutate rapidly.

The situation, in other words, is rather messy, and there's a good chance that you could order two plants with the same name and wind up having two different kinds. Who cares? Both will be attractive additions to your garden, ones that require little care and provide great enjoyment.

For areas where winter lows are within the range of −30° to +30° F.

PLANT SOURCES: Bluestone Perennials, Carroll Gardens, Crownsville Nursery, Primrose Path, Sunlight Gardens, White Flower Farm

SEED SOURCE: Park Seed

The balloon flower is consistently recommended as one of the best perennial flowers. And no wonder. It features a pretty blue color, neat appearance, resistance to pests and diseases, and long life. A single clump of these flowers has been known to bloom for twenty or more summers.

There are, however, four points for the beginning gardener to consider:

1 The plants are easily confused with bellflowers. Indeed, in American gardens at the turn of the century, this was known as the Chinese bellflower. It helps to realize that both flowers are members of the Campanula family, hence the resemblance. The bellflower recommended in this book starts to bloom in June and the balloon flower in July. Try both if you want a long stretch of blue in your garden.

2 It takes a while for the balloon flower to really shine in a garden. If you opt to plant seeds—and balloon flower is easily grown this way—you have to wait two or three years before it will put forth its first blossoms. If you buy young plants, you'll have flowers sooner, but even so you have to wait about three years before a good-size clump is formed.

3 Once settled, balloon flowers do not like to be moved. This means you have to be particularly careful in choosing the site for this plant. It really shines in full sun but will also flower in partial shade. Since its height is about 2 feet, it's best to place the balloon flower in the middle or back row of your flower bed.

4 Balloon flower is a skinny plant. You will need to have other plants nearby to fill up space. When the blue flowers come out, the balloon flower sometimes gets top heavy and needs to be staked.

In summary, this plant requires little work but some patience. It's worth the wait. The blue flowers are lovely on their tall stems in midsummer and add a nice touch of color and elegance to any garden.

BEE
MONARDA DIDYMA
BALM

For areas where winter lows are within the range of −25° to +30° F.

PLANT SOURCES: Primrose Path, Native Gardens, Sunlight Gardens

Bee balm flowers are wonderfully exotic looking. When the petals first unfold, they look like the spikes of a garish punk hairdo. As the seeds form, the petals slowly fall off, creating a flower that looks like the tonsured head of a monk. When the last spark of color has gone, a rich brown ball of seeds is left and this is handsome in dried-flower arrangements.

Up until the last stage, bees are constantly buzzing about the flower, hence its popular name. Hummingbirds are attracted to it also, and if you watch carefully, you might get to see one of these tiny creatures.

The botanical name for this member of the mint family honors Dr. N. Monardez, a Spanish physician and botanist from Seville, who wrote the first book on plants in the New World. The English translation of this book was published in 1577 and was titled *Joyfull Newes out of the newe founde Worlde*.

Indeed, one of the most significant and least heralded effects of the opening of the Americas was the transatlantic crossing of vegetation. The introduction of new plants was "joyful" for Europeans both rich and poor. Gardening activity among wealthy nobles was very active at the time Monardez wrote and the new food introductions enriched many a poor peasant's diet.

Bee balm, which grows wild from Newfoundland to Florida and west to Tennessee and Michigan, became one of the more popular plants. In addition to its adaptability to many temperature variations, it looks attractive and requires little care.

Bee balm grows in sun or semi-shade but looks best in the former. In my garden, I origi-

nally planted it at the back of the border because of its 3-foot height. The plant literally crept forward over a three-year span to the front, where there was more sun. I did notice that as the plant began to receive more sun, the stems tended to remain upright and not fall over, as they were prone to do in the shadier location.

Though it is generally recommended that bee balm be grown in moist, well-drained average soil, it has survived prolonged dry spells in my garden. This plant is supposed to be quite spectacular in waterside gardens, a site I would like to see some day.

I have found that several of my plants will bloom again if I cut the stems before the flowers go to seed. I snip them back to a height of about 1 foot, and a month or so later I am rewarded with some additional flowers, though not in the profusion of the first bloom.

Hot and humid Princeton, New Jersey, is a perfect breeding ground for powdery mildew, and in August bee balms are often covered with this unsightly fungus. When that happens, I just cut the plant to the ground and throw the offending stems away. This treatment is too drastic to encourage a second flowering but it doesn't kill the plant, and by next summer there are gorgeous flowers once more.

My bee balm is a species plant, the kind that grows in the wild. Most large nurseries offer cultivars with names such as "Cambridge Scarlet" or "Adam." From what I gather, the only difference between the cultivars and the species is the shade of red. If you want to try the cultivars, do. If you want to grow the original, you can obtain it from the nurseries listed on page 72.

BLACK-EYED

RUDBECKIA FULGIDA "GOLDSTURM"

SUSAN

For areas where winter lows are within the range of −30° to +30° F.

PLANT SOURCES: Bluestone Perennials, Burpee, Busse Gardens, Canyon Creek Nursery, Carroll Gardens, Crownsville Nursery, Holbrook Farm, J. W. Jung, Lamb Nurseries, Milaeger's Gardens, Piccadilly Farm, Sunlight Gardens, Wayside, White Flower Farm

SEED SOURCES: Park Seed, Thompson & Morgan

This flower is a member of a great all-American group known as black-eyed Susans, or, in horticultural terms, the Rudbeckias. They can be found growing throughout our country, their yellow petals and black centers brightening fields and roadsides everywhere. All told, there are about twenty-five species.

The botanical name is in honor of Olaf Rudbeck, a professor of botany at the University of Uppsala in Sweden in the first part of the eighteenth century. Professor Rudbeck had the good sense to appoint a poor but promising student, Carl Linnaeus, as a deputy lecturer in botany at the university. "Now, through the grace of God," Linnaeus wrote a friend, "I have an income."

Linnaeus went on to develop the first accepted system for naming and classifying plants. There is no doubt that gratitude played a part in his naming a flower after his benefactor, but perhaps another factor was equally important. Professor Rudbeck had twenty-four children—a pretty good feat in the mid-1700s, when infant and maternal mortality rates were quite high. Black-eyed Susans are just as prolific.

Most of the plants we see from highways are *Rudbeckia hirta*. These are generally called half-hardy perennials; that is, they can winter over in some areas but not all. Their cheerful reappearance in the wild every year is due to their great capacity for self-seeding. These sprout in the spring and flower by mid-summer. I really like this plant but, in my garden, it has one glaring weakness: susceptibility to powdery mildew. Once the dusty white spots of this fungus start appearing on the leaves, I know the plant will shrivel in about three weeks. It's rather sad —and ugly to boot.

The plant named here, *Rudbeckia fulgida* *"Goldsturm,"* is much hardier than the roadside version and is not susceptible to mildew. It's been around for over fifty years, having been developed in 1937 by Karl Foerster, a perennial plantsman in Germany.

As a cultivar, however, this particular black-eyed Susan does not always come true from seed and therein lies an interesting story. Many nurseries grow this plant from seed, and the result is more like the species *R. fulgida*—a perennial, durable black-eyed Susan that gets about 3 feet tall and flops over. That description fits the plants in my garden. The cultivar is supposed to be more compact and only 2 feet in height.

Wayside Gardens has been conducting an experiment to discover the difference between the two. Horticulturists at the nursery tracked down a descendant of Foerster's plants in Switzerland and obtained enough seedlings to grow their own from root cuttings. They are also growing "Goldsturm" from seed. The two plants—seed grown and vegetatively produced —are planted side by side in their gardens. The vegetatively grown version cost about 50 percent more than the seed grown.

In the meantime, just about every nursery and garden center offers the plant under the name listed above. The flower you buy might not totally live up to the "Goldsturm" description, but it will still be a colorful, easy care perennial for a sunny or partially shaded garden.

BUTTERFLY

ASCLEPIAS TUBEROSA

WEED

For areas where winter lows are within the range of −30° to +30° F.

PLANT SOURCES: Burpee, Busse Gardens, Carroll Gardens, Crownsville Nursery, Holbrook Farm, Milaeger's Gardens, Native Gardens, Piccadilly Farm, Primrose Path, Sunlight Gardens, Wayside, White Flower Farm

SEED SOURCES: Harris Seed, Park Seed, Thompson & Morgan

The butterfly weed is a handsome plant that can often be seen growing wild in meadows from Mexico through the United States to Canada. Its flowers are fragrant and excellent for cutting. Once established in your garden, butterfly weed will come back year after year without any care.

There's more to this plant than looks and durability, however. It is responsible for the survival of one of our country's prettiest butterflies —the orange-and-black monarch butterfly.

The butterfly weed and the monarch butterfly formed a partnership thousands of years ago, before recorded history. Though the exact origin of the plant cannot be pinpointed, the butterfly weed is an American native. During the last Ice Age, it probably left Canada and the northern half of the United States and moved south as the glaciers advanced. When the plant reached warm areas such as Mexico and southern California, it attracted the attention of the monarch butterfly.

The plant contains chemicals which are poisonous to many insects that prey upon butterflies but not to the butterflies themselves. Through an evolutionary process, the monarch caterpillar learned that if it fed upon the butterfly weed, it could store the plant's poisons in its tissues. In effect, the caterpillar, and then the butterfly itself, became deadly poison to predators that eat them.

Eventually birds and other predators learned that it was in their best interests to avoid the monarch butterfly. The color of the butterfly proclaims its special relationship to the plant.

When the Ice Age ended, the butterfly weed began to move north again. The monarch butterfly followed, but came to recognize that it could not survive northern winters. The evolutionary solution that kept the partnership between plant and insect alive resulted in a remarkable annual migration.

Each year, hundreds of millions of monarch butterflies travel back and forth between Mexico and Canada. The journey is so long, and so time-consuming, that a single butterfly cannot accomplish it. In the spring, millions of monarchs start to move north, breeding as they go.

And throughout the thousands of miles that they travel, the butterfly weed provides the monarchs with food and built-in protection.

In the fall, fifth-generation descendants of the spring monarchs turn around and start heading south. It is presumed that this migration must be genetic. Monarch butterflies in the eastern United States and Canada head for groves of oyamel fir trees located in the mountains of Mexico, while monarchs west of the Rockies travel to groves in southern California.

If you would like to give food and sustenance to the monarch butterfly and, at the same time, have an attractive, easy care perennial in your garden, try the butterfly weed. Since it self-seeds quite readily, I decided to grow it from seed myself. I gave some of the extra seedlings to my neighbor, and these bloomed the first year in her sunny garden. Since my plants are in heavier soil and in part shade, they did not blossom until the following year.

Butterfly weed has a very long taproot. While this gives the plant the ability to resist drought, it does make it difficult to relocate. Pick a spot carefully. Butterfly weed is late to come up in spring, so be careful that you do not disturb its tender shoots when you are clearing the garden at that time.

In July and August, the plant will send up as many as ten stalks crowned with brilliant orange flowers. Up to 2 feet high, the plants look spectacular in flower beds. In the fall, butterfly weed provides another bonus for your garden. It forms 2- to 3-inch canoe-shaped pods that can be used in dried-flower assortments. If left long enough, the pods will open and scatter seeds borne on white, silklike strands.

COREOPSIS

COREOPSIS LANCEOLATA

For areas where winter lows are within the range of −30° to +30° F.

PLANT SOURCES: Carroll Gardens, Native Gardens, Primrose Path, Sunlight Gardens

SEED SOURCE: Harris Seeds

This is a blowsy plant, not at all the sort to be found in a formal garden. Brazenly covered with bright yellow daisylike flowers throughout the heat of high summer, it usually gets so top-heavy that it just sprawls about—and continues to send up more blooms with delicious abandon.

Coreopsis is a native American and, in the wild, cuts a wide swath through the country. You can find it growing on its own from New England to Wisconsin all the way down to Florida and New Mexico. American Indians used it for producing beautiful dyes, and pioneers are supposed to have put its seeds in mattresses as repellants against fleas and bedbugs.

Its first official record in horticultural literature, however, is due to the efforts of Mark Catesby, a renowned eighteenth-century English naturalist. During a trip to Virginia in the early 1700s to visit his sister and brother-in-law, Catesby saw the flower and sent its seed back to Great Britain. There, it was classified as a member of the *Coreopsis* genus.

All of the *Coreopsis* species bear dark seeds that are supposed to resemble ticks, which is why you might sometimes find them referred to as tickseed. The botanical name comes from the Greek and reflects this characteristic: *koris*, for "bug" or "tick," and *opsis*, for "a resemblance."

Though *Coreopsis lanceolata* has been known to gardeners for over 250 years now, it has never been a particularly big hit, either here or in England. Rather, cultivars such as "Baby Sun" or "Sunray" are usually grown because they are more refined—neither falling down nor spreading about.

For an easy care plant, however, it is really hard to go wrong with *C. lanceolata*. It doesn't mind blistering summer heat and will even forgive you for forgetting to water. If you remember to snip off the seed heads, it will bloom abundantly for a good two months. Coreopsis adds a sunny dash of yellow to the garden—and increases quite rapidly. You can divide its clumps whenever you want to and stick the divisions in any other sunny or semi-shaded part of your flower bed that needs cheering up. In addition, this coreopsis is hardier and longer-lived than its more refined relatives.

My friend Sue Fremon gave me my first clump of this plant and said it was one of the best performers in her Princeton garden. It has done well in mine also. While neither of us has had diseases or pests attack this plant, I have read that aphids and fungus can be problems. Perhaps if you grow this coreopsis in the full, hot sun it likes best, these two nuisances will leave it alone.

DAYLILY

HEMEROCALLIS FULVA

For areas where winter lows are within the range of −35° to +25° F.

PLANT SOURCES: Busse Gardens, Crownsville Nursery

The plant pictured here is the tawny daylily, a flower that has been grown in China and Japan for centuries. There, it is valued as much for its usefulness as for its good looks and durability. To this day, the Chinese dry the buds, called *gum-tsoy,* and use them to thicken soups. Other cooks use the spring shoots much as we do as-paragus. The roots are eaten also and are sup-posed to have a nutlike flavor. .

The tawny daylily is sterile; it does not create seed. In order to spread throughout the northern half of our planet, it has had to hitchhike across continents—an amazing performance when you think about it.

The tawny daylily reached Europe in 1576, and quickly proved itself a tough plant that could grow just about anywhere, in sun or partial shade, and under just about any condition. No wonder it was among the plant baggage brought to the New World by early settlers. As these people abandoned their first crude, rough homes for bigger and better places, however, the daylilies were left behind. There's many a lost family history behind an orange-blooming clump that now seems to be growing in untamed wilderness.

There are only sixteen species of daylilies, of which the tawny daylily is one. That's hard to believe, especially when looking through books and catalogues that contain hundreds of illustrations of daylilies. These plants are short, medium, or tall; bloom early or late; and come in an astonishing array of colors. This multiplicity is due to the ease with which daylily hybrids can be created. All that's necessary is to take over a bee's role and bring the pollen from the stamen of one plant to the stigma of another. The resulting seed is saved and planted. Over 27,000 different daylilies have been created this way by both amateur gardeners and professional horticulturists.

This burst of creativity has only occurred within the past sixty years and is primarily due to the work of Dr. A. B. Stout. As a boy growing up in rural Wisconsin, Dr. Stout had been intrigued with the tawny daylily, wondering why it was so prevalent and yet not being able to find any seed. After becoming a botanist, he conducted research on the plant and discovered that it was sterile. The tawny daylily does produce pollen, however, and Dr. Stout used this to fertilize daylilies of other species. Through this program he produced the first pink, red, and clear orange daylilies. Others read his book, the classic *Day Lilies* published in 1934, and went on to create their own daylilies.

Thanks to all this effort, it is now possible to buy daylilies in much the same way as one buys clothes; color, shape, and time of year are all factors to consider. If, however, you want to have a bit of history in your garden and a daylily that is not in the least bit fussy, try the tawny daylily. In a contest for the most easy care perennial, this one would probably win hands down.

FEVERFEW

CHRYSANTHEMUM PARTHENIUM

For areas where winter lows are within the range of −15° to +30° F.

PLANT SOURCES: Carroll Gardens, Milaeger's Gardens

SEED SOURCE: Thompson & Morgan

Fifty years after the Pilgrims landed, John Josselyn published a description of flowers thriving in the new land. "Fetherfew," he wrote, "prospereth exceedingly."

The key to feverfew's great prosperity is the huge number of seeds produced each year. These sprout freely the following spring in sun or partial shade, grow about 2 feet tall, and then burst forth with an abundance of small, daisy-like flowers in mid-July. Feverfew will continue to bloom right through light frosts, and we generally include it in a small flower arrangement for our Thanksgiving dinner.

In Princeton and warmer climates to the south, feverfew not only seeds itself prodigiously but also acts as a perennial, with many of the plants surviving the winter. These take off with the first warmth of spring and reach heights of over 3 feet. Blooming in mid- to late

June, their white blossoms seem to float about the garden, giving the whole setting the appearance of being filled with miniature white dogwoods. I cut masses of bouquets from these plants and still more side shoots come forth to bloom in their turn. Flowers that I don't cut form seed for the next year's generation.

The only pest I have ever seen to even remotely bother feverfew is the four-lined plant bug. You can tell it has been at work when you see little brown spots appear all over the leaves. A quick dusting of rotenone dispatches that problem.

The Pilgrims, it should be noted, did not bring feverfew to this country because of its good looks and ease of care. Rather, it was an important medicinal herb used, as its popular name indicates, to cure fevers and a host of other ailments.

In 1597, the English surgeon and garden writer John Gerard wrote in his general history of plants that feverfew was also effective in treating migraine headaches. Sufferers of this affliction would eat the pungent, bitter leaves for a period of weeks and would notice a sharp decrease of attacks and, in some cases, a total cure.

This old-fashioned migraine remedy was rediscovered in Europe and began to appear in newspaper articles about ten years ago. Scientists in Great Britain conducted experiments to test the validity of such a treatment, and in an August 1985 article in the *British Medical Journal,* three researchers concluded that there was indeed evidence that feverfew can prevent migraine attacks.

Here we have a plant that is extremely good looking, requires the absolute minimum amount of care, and provides a health benefit. One would think it would be on everybody's most-wanted list and yet it is extremely difficult to find.

Part of the problem lies with its botanical name. Botanists have had a difficult time clas-

sifying this plant. *Hortus Third* says it is a member of the *Chrysanthemum* genus (the only member, incidentally, that prefers average to poor soil). The British researchers identify it as *Tanacetum parthenium,* and many nurseries offer it as *Matricaria parthenium.* To further muddy things for an already confused gardener, there are varieties of *Matricaria* that are called feverfew, look somewhat like feverfew, but have nowhere near the durability, ease of care, and length of bloom of the *Chrysanthemum parthenium.*

This plant is a personal favorite of mine, and I was pleased to find it offered by the nurseries listed on this page. Only Carroll Gardens presents its correct name, however. Milaeger's Gardens lists it as *Matricaria* "Ultra Double White" and Thompson & Morgan places it in the Herb section of their catalogue as "Parthenium Matricaria." Fortunately, once you obtain this plant it will seed itself so prolifically and look so handsome that you won't have to worry about its botanical name ever again.

GOOSENECK

LYSIMACHIA CLETHROIDES

PLANT

For areas where winter lows are within the range of −25° to +15° F.

PLANT SOURCES: Bluestone Perennials, Canyon Creek Nursery, Carroll Gardens, Crownsville Nursery, Holbrook Farm, Milaeger's Gardens, Piccadilly Farm, White Flower Farm

SEED SOURCE: Thompson & Morgan

Gooseneck plant gets its popular name from the odd-shaped white flowers that it produces every year. Though the name doesn't sound very elegant, the flowers do have a touch of class about them and look rather striking in the garden. They bloom for about six weeks, and after they fade, the flower bed is left with a nice 2-foot clump of dark green foliage.

A native of Japan and China, gooseneck plant is sometimes called Japanese loosestrife and can now be found in gardens from coast to coast in our country. It's a great plant for the middle row of your flower bed. Put something like a purple New York aster—which is shorter and blooms later—in front of it and a tall, thin plant such as an orange tiger lily behind it.

Under the right conditions, this plant can almost take over a garden. One book suggests planting it with daylilies and letting the two struggle for space, with neither being able to overwhelm the other. Right conditions for a gooseneck plant mean average moist soil and, in southern regions, some shade.

In my garden, the gooseneck plant is not at all invasive. Indeed, I wondered if the clump I received from a neighbor would even survive the first year once the slugs finished feasting on it. Tough flower that it is, the gooseneck plant did come back the next year and the size of the clump increased slightly. Nevertheless, heavy soil, only partial sun, and continued slug attacks all combine to keep this a rather restrained plant.

Aside from the slugs, no other pests or diseases have bothered this plant in my garden and I cannot find mention of any in garden literature. Four-lined plant bugs launched a massive attack in my neighbor Jean Woodward's garden, but she dispatched them quickly, with a dusting of rotenone.

Nature sees to the gooseneck plant's watering requirements and it does not need staking. On its part, the plant provides exotic blooms that add interest to many cut-flower arrangements. This is such a low-key, easy care plant that it is not surprising to find that it is one of the more popular perennials offered by nurseries in this book.

LYTHRUM

LYTHRUM SALICARIA "MORDEN PINK"

For areas where winter lows are within the range of −30° to +35° F.

PLANT SOURCES: Burpee, Carroll Gardens, Crownsville Nursery, Holbrook Farm, J. W. Jung, Lamb Nurseries, Wayside

This plant is the victim of bad press, condemned unfairly by name only and not on actual

peformance. "Morden Pink" lythrum is a cultivar, a specially created plant that is sterile. Since it does not provide seed, it can only increase by spreading its roots and these branch out rather slowly. "Morden Pink" is a most restrained plant and is not considered invasive in the least.

Lythrum salicaria, or purple loosestrife, the plant from which "Morden Pink" was developed, is another matter. This European import has just about taken over wetlands across the northern part of our country. Its tall spikes, covered with rich purple flowers, make spectacular summer displays.

What looks good from a distance, however, becomes dismaying at closer inspection. Purple loosestrife is so aggressive in its spread that it is choking out other vegetation and endangering animal species that depend on that vegetation for survival. The state legislature of Wisconsin deemed this such a serious matter that it banned the sale of lythrum within its borders. The legislation is so worded that even sterile cultivars are not allowed to enter the state.

This is a shame. "Morden Pink" has all the good traits and none of the bad of purple loosestrife. As this book went to press, plant breeders and nursery people were trying to see if the law could be amended to allow the sale of sterile cultivars of lythrum.

"Morden Pink" is 3 feet tall and a most attractive plant that can grow in either full sun or light shade. Its long, thin spikes start to bloom in July and continue looking elegant right through August. This lythrum will grow in most any kind of soil but will spread faster in a moist, wetland setting.

This plant attracts no pests or diseases, and about the only work that is required is cutting the dead stalks after they are killed by frosts. This can be done during either a fall or spring cleaning; it does make for a neater garden if done in the fall.

PERENNIAL AGERATUM

EUPATORIUM COELESTINUM

MIST FLOWER

For areas where winter lows are within the range of −10° to +20° F.

PLANT SOURCES: Carroll Gardens, Crownsville Nursery, Holbrook Farm, Milaeger's Gardens, Native Gardens, Sunlight Gardens

Perennial ageratum is a member of an up-and-coming group in the plant world. The genus name is *Eupatorium* and most of its members, bearing the rather unglamorous popular name of Joe-Pye weed, are commonly found growing along roadsides.

To date, perennial ageratum is the only one of this group to find some degree of acceptance among gardeners. Its positive attributes are many: it easily weathers heat and drought; it blooms in August, adding a much welcome touch of blue to the late summer garden; its 2-to 3-foot-tall green foliage is handsome; and it is a long bloomer, with its flowers appearing for almost a month. As garden writer Allen Lacy has noted, "Whoever decided to turn it from a wildflower into a garden plant deserves a prize."

The one serious drawback to this plant is that its roots spread with complete abandon in warm, sandy soils. Pamela Harper, a well-known garden writer and photographer, had to remove it from her Virginia garden because new shoots kept cropping up in unwanted places.

Since my perennial ageratum grows in rather heavy soil in semi-shade, I have not had this problem. I do, however, dig out many of its roots during my spring garden-cleaning and leave only a rather small spot devoted to this plant. By August, it has outgrown this area—which was my intention—and looks just great near the back of the garden.

The only problem I have had with perennial ageratum is an attack by the four-lined plant bug. This becomes obvious when the leaves are covered with small brown spots, where the bug has sucked them dry. One or two dustings with rotenone takes care of this matter.

I have read that perennial ageratum can be stricken with various forms of rot. In fact, one clump disappeared rather mysteriously one year and perhaps that was the cause. Nevertheless, by having plants spaced throughout my garden I am always assured that one will be in a mood to spread and I can transplant the green shoots from these roots to areas where I would like them.

Nurseries and plant breeders in the two Germanies—both East and West—have taken an immense shine to native American perennials and are busy developing new cultivars. The *Eupatorium* genus has come under rather sharp scrutiny and you can expect to see many new introductions touting their virtues. These are always more expensive than the proven old-timers. If your garden budget is limited and you want a nice, care-free touch of blue in your August garden, consider *Eupatorium coelestinum*, the perennial ageratum.

PURPLE

ECHINACEA PURPUREA

CONEFLOWER

For areas where winter lows are within the range of −30° to +30° F.

PLANT SOURCES: Bluestone Perennials, Carroll Gardens, Holbrook Farm, Milaeger's Gardens, Native Gardens, Piccadilly Farm, Primrose Path, Sunlight Gardens

SEED SOURCE: Harris Seeds

Purple coneflower, an American native of the Midwest, is a gorgeous plant that was often found in perennial gardens at the turn of the century. Somehow, despite its good looks, it lost favor during the years and has just recently started to make a comeback.

Though one garden writer has commented that it could hardly be improved upon, breeders have disagreed and come out with several cultivars bearing names such as "Bright Star" and "White Lustre." Generally, these cultivars are offered by the larger nurseries and the true—or species—purple coneflower by smaller nurseries, often in the back of their catalogues under the wildflower sections.

While there is no doubt that purple coneflower looks handsome growing on the prairies, there is nothing wild about its appearance in a flower bed. In fact, it is rather regal with its long purple petals and burnished brown cones on stems reaching to 5 feet. And it continues to look grand for a long period, up to two months in many gardens.

Here are three points in its favor: (1) it is one of the least expensive perennials in this book, selling in most cases for $3 or less per plant; (2) it lasts for a long time in cut-flower arrangements; and (3) even when all the petals fall off, the cones still look good and are often used in dried-flower arrangements.

Growing requirements for the purple coneflower are few. Plant it in full sun or light shade in just about any kind of soil, except that which is soggy (wet soil in winter will kill the plant). Should the flower reach 5 feet in height, as it often does in full sun, it may have to be staked.

Purple coneflower spreads very slowly and only needs to be divided every four years or so. That's just about all the work you have to do. The plant tolerates drought, so you don't have to water it.

My purple coneflower was a gift from a neighbor, Mickey Eggers. She spends a lot of time ensuring that the soil in her garden is rich and loamy, the kind you see in garden books. Her purple coneflower grows in this environment and under full sun. It is huge, handsome, and in need of staking. The clump that Mickey gave me was placed in clay soil with partial shade—not as nice a home as it had before. As a result, the plant only reaches 2 feet and does not need to be staked.

I have read that purple coneflower is prone to attack by Japanese beetles. These pests have yet to discover my plants, possibly because they are so busy feasting on my sundrops. In any case, Japanese beetles have not been a problem but slugs have. They crawl out of the nearby green-and-white hosta leaves and nibble on the purple coneflower. The plant manages to out-grow these pests, however, and puts forth lovely flowers in the summer.

ROSE

LYCHNIS CORONARIA

CAMPION

For areas where winter lows are within the range of −35° to +25° F.

PLANT SOURCES: Carroll Gardens, Crownsville Nursery, Lamb Nurseries

This native of the Mediterranean region and central Asia is a true old-fashioned plant. Its foliage is soft and silvery gray, creating an appearance that has earned it the nickname of Dusty Miller. There's nothing dusty about its

flowers, however. These are an intense magenta and really spark up a garden.

Historical records indicate that rose campion was grown in European gardens at least as far back as the fourteenth century. It had some practical use in those days, for the down on the leaves was used to make lampwicks. Early Americans must have also liked this flower; its seeds were offered for sale in a March 30, 1760, Boston advertisement.

Whoever responded to that ad would have had to wait two summers for the rose campion to bloom. The first year it produces soft gray mats of foliage and some gardeners grow it for this reason alone; it looks handsome as an edging plant and even winters over. In the second year, stems up to 2 feet high emerge and are covered with 1-inch flowers.

After the first rush is over, the plant puts forth a blossom or two throughout the rest of the summer. The stems get so spindly, however, that I usually cut them back to the ground.

When I snip the stems, the former flower heads are filled with small black seeds. I shake these around the garden, and by early September there are many new seedlings all set to bloom the next year. That's how easy it is to ensure a continuous supply of these flowers.

Given its ease of care, the fact that few diseases or pests bother the plant, and that it can grow in just about any soil in sun or part shade, it's easy to see why rose campion was a popular plant. What is difficult to fathom, however, is why it fell out of favor. In 1901, Alice Morse Earle was writing in her book on *Old Time Gardens* that, "I have never heard any one speak of this plant with special affection or admiration."

Perhaps some people disliked the brightness of the color or the fact that it spreads so easily —for any number of reasons, this plant almost faded from public view. It is, I suppose, all a matter of taste. For my part, I think it's great.

ROSE

MALVA ALCEA "FASTIGIATA"

MALLOW

For areas where winter lows are within the range of −20° to +30° F.

PLANT SOURCES: Bluestone Perennials, Carroll Gardens, Crownsville Nursery, Holbrook Farm, Milaeger's Gardens, Wayside, White Flower Farm

SEED SOURCES: Park Seed, Thompson & Morgan

The rose mallow is like the traditional bridesmaid: a stalwart member of the bridal party but never the feature attraction. While this is a wonderful easy care flower, no one seems to get very excited about it.

Fortunately, my friend Joyce Boyle thought it would be a perfect match for me. While Joyce enjoys the challenge of gardening, she knows that I am basically indolent and do not. Whenever she finds a plant that can grow in any kind of soil, in full sun or part shade, and without the use of pesticides, she immediately thinks of me. Such was the case with rose mallow.

I planted a small self-sown seedling from Joyce's garden in my rear flower bed one sunny afternoon in May, and by August it had formed a handsome green backdrop, one covered with soft pink flowers that continued to bloom until the end of September. Each subsequent year, the clump from the original plant has gotten larger. Eventually, I have read, I can expect it to send up as many as fifty stems in one season.

Now that it has settled in—and rose mallows have long taproots and do not like to be disturbed—the plant starts blooming earlier, usually in July, while continuing to produce flowers well into September and sometimes even into early October. It grows a good 5 feet tall.

Rose mallow should be staked, but this is really a simple matter. If it is growing next to a fence (and the plant looks quite handsome against wood panels), just circle the foliage with garden string and tie it to the fence.

Rose mallow is a European wildflower and was grown in British gardens at the turn of the century. I have yet to discover who developed the cultivar "Fastigiata," but it has proved so popular that the species plant is not offered by major nurseries.

Unlike many cultivars, however, 'Fastigiata' does produce seed that runs true; that is, seed that produces plants similar to the parent. Indeed, 'Fastigiata' produces a lot of seeds, and I not only have many plants now lining the back of the flower border but also have given away quite a few to friends and neighbors. If you find these seedlings a nuisance, they are easily pulled out of the garden during spring or fall clean-up.

STOKESIA

STOKESIA LAEVIS

CORNFLOWER

For areas where winter lows are within the range of −10° to +30° F.

PLANT SOURCES: Burpee, Sunlight Gardens, Piccadilly Farm, White Flower Farm

At the beginning of this century, garden writer Louise Shelton commented that stokesia should be seen more often in gardens. One can make the same remark today. While this is a favorite in its native haunts in the southeastern part of the United States, it has not really gained national recognition. This is long overdue.

Stokesia produces large, blue, asterlike flowers that are handsome in the garden and great in cut-flower arrangements. The leaves are a nice, deep green and, in my garden, remain as low clumps over winter. In spring, the 1- to 2-foot-tall stems shoot up and need to be staked. While no other writer comments on the necessity for this task, my stokesias fall over if not buttressed; perhaps this is so because my soil is poor.

Stokesia's blooming period varies according to its surroundings. In Princeton, the plants are loaded with flowers in July. I cut these off before they go to seed—dead heading is the garden term—and then have new flowers in late August and September. In southern California, stokesia is supposed to bloom intermittently all year; and in Florida, it blooms in the winter. In stokesia's native Southeast, it blooms heavily in June and then sporadically through frost.

There appears to be unanimous agreement that stokesia is an easy care plant and, because of its blue color, an attractive addition to any garden. It will grow in full sun or partial shade. While it prefers moist soil, it is tough enough to withstand drought. Soggy soil in the winter can kill it, however, and it is best to mulch this plant where there are severe frost heaves.

I could find no written record of any diseases or pests bothering this plant. Experience, however, has proved otherwise. I have a lot of spider mites—awful things that are barely visible to the naked eye and that suck juices from plant leaves. These mites leave tiny pinlike pricks on the stokesia leaves but the plant is so strong that it resists the attack. It does require a bit of extra watering, however, to replenish the moisture drained by the spider mites. When doing so, I spray full force on the leaves with the hose; this serves as a nonpoisonous pest control by washing away many of the mites.

I actually have two different stokesias. One is a cultivar and the other is a species plant. To be honest, I cannot tell the difference between the two. This is another example, I feel, where budget-minded gardeners should opt for the less-expensive plant if given a choice between a species and a cultivar. Only a truly discerning eye can tell the difference. You can save even more money by growing this plant from seed, which is very easy to do.

TIGER

LILIUM TIGRINUM

LILY

For areas where winter lows are within the range of −30° to +15° F.

BULB SOURCES: Piccadilly Farm, Wayside

Tiger lilies have been cultivated by the Chinese for over a thousand years, making these lovely plants one of the world's oldest gardening flowers. An East India Company officer, Captain Kirkpatrick, saw them growing in China in 1804 and sent some bulbs back to the botanical garden at Kew. It was almost a case of love at first sight, and the English have remained enamoured of these ever since.

Plantsmen quickly discovered that hybrids could be developed by crossing the tiger lily with other lilies. Hundreds of new varieties were created. Today, with careful planning, it is possible to have lilies blooming in the garden from early June until frost. These come in many different shapes and colors, and the heights range from less than 2 feet to a good 8 feet.

Many of the hybrids, however, do have special planting requirements and are susceptible to diseases. Most are not for easy care gardeners. The tiger lily is.

The tiger lily is a sturdy, dependable plant that has actually become a wildflower in some parts of the eastern United States. In my garden, it gets about 4 feet tall, although I have read elsewhere that its height is anywhere from 2 to 5 feet. My tiger lilies grow in poor soil in partial shade but would do equally well—if not better—in full sun.

This plant is supposed to be immune to pests and diseases. Indeed, with regard to the latter, it is actually a carrier of—though not detrimentally affected by—a mosaic disease that can devastate other lilies. If you want to put forth a bit of extra effort and have a variety of lilies in your garden, do not include the tiger lily because it could harm the others.

With regard to pests, something occasionally attacks the leaves of my tiger lily; they appear eaten at the ends with a bit of yellow blotching. This doesn't stop the plant from producing its famous orange and black polka-dot blooms. Wayside Gardens says that these plants will bear up to forty blossoms; again probably because my growing conditions and care are far from ideal, my plants only put forth ten to fifteen. Because my plant is 4 feet tall, it does need staking.

The tiger lily is actually a sterile plant, in that is does not produce seed. It does better, however. It produces little black bulbils at the junction of its leaves and stem. These can be planted. Often, they fall off the stem and plant themselves, which is why you will find extra tiger lilies in your garden over the years. These new plantings produce flowers in two or three years.

In Japan, tiger lily bulbs are cooked and eaten. They are supposed to taste somewhat like artichokes, but I cannot vouch for that— nor do I have any intention of trying to.

YARROW

ACHILLEA MILLEFOLIUM

For areas where winter lows are within the range of −40° to +30° F.

PLANT SOURCES: Crownsville Nursery, Native Gardens, Sunlight Gardens

SEED SOURCE: Harris Seeds

Garden writers, plant breeders, and nursery people alike scorn this plant as common and invasive. Rather, they prefer the elegant new hybrids and cultivars that are being developed —handsome plants with names such as 'Coronation Gold,' 'Moonshine,' and 'Red Beauty.'

While I will not gainsay the merits of these newly arrived yarrows, I would like to say a word in favor of the original version. This is a plant that is best grown in poor to average soil —just the kind of setting a new gardener often confronts. It is so tough and adaptable that it has traveled unharmed throughout most of the world, originating in Europe and western Asia and now naturalized as a weed in North America, Australia, and New Zealand.

It is an ancient plant that emerged in prehistoric times and became the fabric of legend when it was named botanically after Achilles. That young warrior is supposed to have used it during the Trojan War to stanch bleeding wounds.

It was so esteemed during the Roman Empire that it was one of the herbs drawn and described in a manuscript compiled in 400 A.D. This manuscript was translated by an English monk during the eleventh century, and it is uncanny to look at his illustrated manuscript and see the very same yarrow that grows by our roadsides today.

Many other cultures and societies also used yarrow as a medicinal plant. During the late sixteenth century, the English herbalist John Gerard advocated chewing a leaf of this plant to relieve toothaches. European folk wisdom decreed that it could help cure baldness. During the nineteenth century in this country, it was listed in medical books.

Though recent research has found that there are chemicals in yarrow that assist blood clotting, the plant is otherwise disdained as a health aid. Perhaps this loss of status and its obvious abandon in sprawling about waysides and fields led to its banishment from proper flower gardens.

If your garden soil is nothing special, and if sunshine falls on it at least five hours a day, consider this yarrow. It has lovely, green fernlike foliage; tidy white flowers on stems 2 to 3 feet tall; and a bloom period of two months or more. I find it necessary to stake my plants—a simple chore that takes all of three minutes. I just push the stake in the ground, prop the yarrow next to it, and then tie it gently with green garden string.

This is one of the few white perennials in my flower beds, and it adds a quiet accent to the garden scheme. It is long lasting as a cut flower and is very easy to dry. Just snip the stem, hang it upside down in a dry, dark place—such as an attic—for about two weeks, and then put the dried flower head in your arrangement.

FALL

FIVE

A delicate color scheme, featuring whites, pinks, and lavenders, can float through the fall garden. The easy care plants here—anemone, boltonia, New York aster, and obedient plant—will rise above the red, yellow, and orange carpeting of fall leaves.

Fall-blooming flowers are nature's goodbye gift to the garden. With the bleakness of winter about to descend, these brightly colored plants assume a precious quality.

There are two kinds of perennials that add color to flower beds from September to hard frosts. The first are the hangers-on—plants that have been blooming during the summer and just don't know when to give up. Five mentioned in earlier chapters will still be doing their best to please you: the violet-blue aster frikartii, the yellow black-eyed Susan, the snowy-white feverfew, the lovely gray foliage of the silver king, and the deep blue spiderwort.

Depending on your growing conditions, eight other plants might also be contributors to your garden, adding red, blues, pinks, and whites to its palette. These easy care perennials are bee balm, bleeding heart, chives, mountain bluet, perennial ageratum, rose mallow, stokesia, and yarrow.

The second group consists of the newcomers. They add welcome variety and new colors to the garden landscape. These plants are described in this chapter.

Fall chrysanthemums are not included in this book. Though they grow easily in the thousands of pots that are sold at grocery stores, garden centers, and school fund-raisers, they are not easy care plants for the garden. They require good, fertile soil; have insect and disease problems; and need to be pinched back several times to encourage bloom and bushiness. I like chrysanthemums and, in fact, have them in my garden. But I opt for the lazy approach—I just buy several pots and place these in bare spots that need a bit of touching up. Once these pot plants have finished blooming, I throw them away.

The first invigorating hints of cold breezes to come are also a sign that it's time to do a bit of fall cleaning. With an easy care garden, you can forget about special bundling-up chores to protect plants during winter months. All that is necessary is a general weeding (to make up for neglect during the summer) and a ruthless cleaning out of any sick or diseased plants. This work can probably be completed in just one nice, sunny fall afternoon. You'll find it pays off by reducing chores the following year.

While you're working outside at this time of year, you will probably find that many plants have become perfect candidates for dried-flower arrangements. All you have to do is cut the stems with the seed heads intact and bring them inside.

If you feel really ambitious in the fall, you might plant more bulbs for the spring. If not, relax and enjoy the flowers described on the following pages.

ANEMONE

ANEMONE VITIFOLIA "ROBUSTISSIMA"

For areas where winter lows are within the range of −20° to +30° F.

PLANT SOURCES: Bluestone Perennials, Busse Gardens, Carroll Gardens, Lamb Nurseries, Milaeger's Gardens, Piccadilly Farm; Wayside

This plant is truly adaptable: it was discovered almost 200 years ago in the mountains of Nepal and now thrives in the heat and humidity of Georgia. It's tough, hardy, elegant, and, perhaps best of all, a gorgeous bloomer in the fall garden.

Its foliage and lovely pink-blushed flowers are very similar to those of flowers called the Japanese anemone *(A. japonica).* The "Robustissima" anemone, however, is most able to handle heat, cold, sun, and drought and can thus be grown in a wider area of our country. This fall anemone is the one for an easy care garden.

Under the right conditions—a rich, moist, humus soil and some late-afternoon shading—this plant can spread like wildfire. Given its good looks, that would not be a catastrophe. It has handsome leaves (they resemble those of grape plants, hence its popular name of grape-leaf anemone), which form nice big clumps during the first part of summer. As the days start to shorten, stems up to 3 feet high become loaded with blossoms. These bloom for almost a month —from mid-September to mid-October in Princeton.

My anemone has yet to spread far because it is rooted in rather dry, heavy soil that only gets about five hours sun in midday. Slugs hide under its leaves and make periodic raids. These conditions probably all combine to keep my plant in its assigned garden space. I do absolutely nothing for it and wonderful specimen that it is, it just keeps producing pretty flowers year after year.

The "Robustissima" anemone is gracious enough to provide an added bonus once it has finished blooming. The seed pods open up and display a delicate white fluff that is great in cut-flower arrangements. I just cut off the already dried stems with the opened seed pods and place them directly into an arrangement.

BOLTONIA

BOLTONIA ASTEROIDES "SNOWBANK"

For areas where winter lows are within the range of −30° to +30° F.

PLANT SOURCES: Bluestone Perennials, Burpee, Canyon Creek Nursery, Carroll Gardens, Holbrook Farm, Milaeger's Gardens, Primrose Path, Wayside, White Flower Farm

After growing quietly in the wild for centuries, boltonia has suddenly burst upon the perennial garden scene. It is the "in" plant to have in flower borders. The story of its unexpectedly swift rise to preeminence contains some of the drama associated with soap operas.

The tale begins two centuries ago, when boltonia was discovered in the eastern United States and named after an eighteenth-century English botanist, James Bolton. It was brought back to England and did not generate any excitement at all. Americans, for their part, were much too busy exploring a continent to care about this member of the aster family.

Boltonia has a rather refined, grayish green foliage that reaches up to 6 feet in height. In the fall, it is covered with daisylike flowers that bloom for well over a month, remaining undaunted by early frosts. Boltonias are tough plants, coping with both cold winters in the north and humid summers in the south.

Give boltonias moist, sandy soil and full sun, and you might have more than you want. In addition, once the blossoms open, the plant becomes top-heavy and usually flops over. Perhaps these two factors account for the fact that boltonias just never found favor in either British or American gardens.

Now the plot thickens: About ten or fifteen years ago someone discovered a shorter version of this plant. It grew only 4 feet high, was loaded with flowers in the fall, and never needed staking. When these plants were lined up in a row, they formed the equivalent of a white hedge.

The new version was aptly named "Snowbank" and was championed by various plant

lovers, among them the New England Wild-flower Society. This prestigious institution brought it to the attention of the horticulturists at White Flower Farm; that nursery began to offer it in spring of 1984. Once White Flower Farm had blessed this plant, other nurseries examined its merits and found it wonderful. Today it tops many lists of great perennials.

Boltonia's meteoric ascent up the popularity poll, however, has proved to be a case of too much too soon. Somewhere along the line somebody goofed and, as one nurseryman describes it, "an imposter snuck in." Many boltonias are now being sold under false pretenses. Rather than being the cultivar "Snowbank," they are instead the species plant—a wildflower

that grows up to 6 feet tall and that falls over when it starts to bloom.

The boltonia in my garden, I fear, is an imposter though it bore a "Snowbank" label at the garden center where it was bought. I like it nevertheless. When it starts to lurch, I simply stick a garden stake in the middle of its growing area and let it lean against that. In return for such a miniscule amount of work, the plant blooms for almost two months—from early September to the end of October. A Princeton friend of mine who has an elegant garden also bought a falsely labeled plant and said she thought its weedy appearance not at all impressive. The plant is no longer in her flower beds.

How can you tell if you are getting the real thing? This is one of the few instances when it is probably best *not* to buy from a local garden center. Most of these stores purchase their plants through wholesalers and do not guarantee the accuracy of the labeling. Your best bet is to buy from a reputable mail-order nursery, one that provides refunds. Many of these nurseries grow their own plants and can vouch that they do indeed offer the "Snowbank" version. If you find you have an imposter—a boltonia that grows close to 6 feet tall and that needs staking in the fall—you can rightfully demand your money back. Or, you can relax as I did, and enjoy the wild version.

NEW YORK

ASTER NOVI-BELGII

ASTER

For areas where winter lows are within the range of −25° to +30° F.

PLANT SOURCES: Burpee, Busse Gardens, Carroll Gardens, Milaeger's Gardens, White Flower Farm

The New York aster had to go to finishing school in England to become respectable. The original grows wild along the eastern coast of North America, from Newfoundland to Georgia. It was sent to England in 1710 and deemed a not very impressive species. At the beginning of this century, however, an English nurseryman named Ernest Ballard took an interest in it and the rest, as the saying goes, is history.

Ballard bred a splendid spectrum of New York asters—plants that range in color from white to crimson to purple, and in height from 8 inches to 36 inches. Thanks to his initiative, there are now hundreds of New York asters to choose from. Many, such as 'Ada Ballard' and 'Patricia Ballard' are the direct result of Ernest Ballard's work and were named by him in honor of members of his family.

In England, these plants bloom in late September, around the feast of St. Michael. They quickly became known as Michaelmas daisies and are extremely popular in that country. The renowned garden writer and designer Gertrude Jekyll used these asters to start the fashion for gardens limited to one color. In Miss Jekyll's case, she created a garden limited not only by color but by season of bloom.

The botanical identification—*novi-belgii*—can be confusing until one reviews early American history. New York was first settled by the Dutch; the plant name recognizes this fact, since Holland was once part of a Roman province called Belgica.

My New York aster came from the garden of a friend living in Barrington, Rhode Island. Unfortunately, she could not recall the cultivar name. As shown in the picture, it has a violet-colored flower with a small yellow center. It grows about 18 inches tall and occasionally flops; even when it does, I do not bother staking it. It spreads quickly, and I transplant it at my whim throughout the growing season. I know that wherever I put it, it will blaze with a welcome burst of color in late August and the first few weeks of September.

All the nurseries listed on this page sell New York asters. Choose a plant on the basis of what height and color best suit your garden design, and then enjoy its prolific and colorful flowers.

OBEDIENT
PHYSOSTEGIA VIRGINIANA
PLANT

For areas where winter lows are within the range of −35° to +35° F.

PLANT SOURCES: Native Gardens, Sunlight Gardens

SEED SOURCES: Harris Seeds, Thompson & Morgan

Obedient plant does not always live up to its popular name. Supposedly, you can bend the stem of each snapdragonlike flower and it will stay in the new position you have given it. My plants tend to snap back impudently. Given their striking good looks in the fall garden, I am more than willing to tolerate their uppityness.

Obedient plant grows wild throughout eastern North America, from New Brunswick to Minnesota, south to Missouri and South Carolina. It was discovered in 1683 and has grown in English gardens for 300 years. It has long been popular in this country, too.

In a book written in 1912, Louise Shelton of Morristown, New Jersey, described obedient plant as a good, and cheap, candidate for the perennial border. Its low cost, she explained, is due to its being included in the category of "Plants Obtainable From Other Gardens." "Every year," she wrote, "there are many perennials in old gardens that must be thinned out and gardeners are glad to dispose of them."

Obedient plant more than fits this description.

Indeed, obedient plant is often described as a highly invasive plant—breaking all border rules and traveling throughout gardens with moist, light soil. It is very restrained in my garden, however, because I have planted it in rather heavy, claylike soil.

As a wildflower, obedient plant is found in semi-shade but it will also do well in full sun. It has no special requirements. And while I have read that it is supposed to have occasional problems with rust disease, this has not been the case in my garden. If I remember to pinch it back early in the summer, much as one is supposed to do with chrysanthemums, there are more branches and flowers. If I forget, I still have a great plant for the fall garden, albeit one that is a bit spindly.

People who like to putter with plants have found this one amenable to tinkering. Several cultivars are offered and they come with names such as "Vivid" and "Summer Snow." These named varieties supposedly have brighter colors but you tend to pay more for the privilege of owning them. I have the original—or species—plant and it does just fine.

SEDUM

SEDUM SPECTABILE

For areas where winter lows are within the range of −30° to +30° F.

PLANT SOURCE: Primrose Path

Depending on the book you read, this plant is native to China, Korea, or Japan. Let us just say it is from eastern Asia. It was brought to Europe about 200 years ago and quickly became a garden favorite because of its looks, durability, and ease of care.

The plant grown in my garden and described here is the old-fashioned species plant. It is descended from sedums located in Dodge City, Kansas, where my father grew up. When he and my stepmother were visiting some of Dad's high school friends, they were given a clump to take as a remembrance of the trip. My stepmother planted it in their Albuquerque, New Mexico, garden, where it quickly became a favorite plant.

Dorothy then passed it on to me when I was out west for an Easter visit. She dug some stems with a little bit of root on each, wrapped them with a wet paper towel, put them in a plastic bag, and assured me that if I took them back on the plane to Princeton, they would bloom that summer.

She was right. The sedum has thrived and has increased through self-seeding and the thickening of clumps. Each year, the light green succulent foliage starts to emerge in early spring and then grows to about 2 feet. The foliage is handsome and in late August and early September the blossoms turn to a brilliant pink. Butterflies and especially bees hover about these flowers all day. The flowers look great in arrangements.

Sedum is supposed to be completely free from pests. Some ignorant creature was unaware of this last summer and proceeded to nibble at the end of the fleshy leaves. The harm was slight, and the sedum looked as spectacular as ever in September.

For obvious sentimental reasons, I am quite fond of this plant. Therefore, I have not tried the very popular hybrid 'Autumn Joy.' This is the sedum usually offered by nurseries, a plant that is often described as one of the top ten perennials grown in the United States. It was developed by Georg Arends, the plantsman who gave the gardening world the *arendsii* astilbes at the beginning of this century. From what I have read, the main difference between this and my sedum is that the flowers on "Autumn Joy" turn a rosy-red before becoming a rust-brown.

If you want to try the highly recommended "Autumn Joy," you will probably find it at your local garden center or in most garden catalogues. It is a very popular plant, and deservedly so. If, however, you want to see what the original is like, you can order it from the Primrose Path.

PUTTING
IT ALL
TOGETHER

SIX

Y ou've picked the site for your garden and you have a good idea of what plants you like. Now what? If you've read Chapter One and reviewed the material on soil and sun requirements, skip to the next heading. If you haven't read that part of the book or have simply forgotten what you did read, pay close attention to the next three paragraphs.

First, take a closer look at your proposed garden site. Are there weeds and grass growing there now? If so, the soil should be fine for your easy care perennials. If not, you probably should have the soil tested. Just put several small samples of dirt into plastic lunch bags, and go to a nearby garden center or county cooperative extension office for information on how you can have your soil analyzed. They will either do it for you or send it to the proper place to get it done.

Second, remember that most plants in this book are best grown in relatively poor soil. "Poor" in this case means soil that is not overly fertilized and a bit on the thick, claylike side. Given extra fertilizer and the addition of peat moss and other organic matter, many of the plants would spread too rapidly and would no longer qualify as easy care. Unless you are inheriting a well-maintained garden, the chances are that your soil is not overly rich.

Third, check the sunlight that the area receives. Try to envision this for an entire growing season. A sunny spot in early spring, for example, can turn quite shady in May or June when the leaves on a nearby maple tree come out. Plants have different light requirements, and this is a crucial factor in deciding which ones would be most suitable for your garden.

With the above three steps out of the way, you are ready to start bringing your garden to life.

BAD NEWS FIRST: BE PREPARED FOR HEARTACHE

Unless you hire a professional landscape firm to do your garden, you must be prepared for meager results in the beginning. After looking at sumptuous pictures and hearing all about "easy care," that's a bit hard to take.

The plain truth is that a garden does not come into being in one fell swoop. It takes time to evolve to a point where you like it. That's why it's best to start small. You can get some idea of a design in a fairly short time period, and you can fill in the bare spots rather quickly and easily.

Take at look at the picture on this page, which shows a garden started by Leslie Peirce two years prior to the writing of this book. Leslie selected a 37 by 3½-foot site next to the fence in her backyard. There had been grass and weeds in the area before, which meant the soil was suitable for a garden. Nevertheless, the ground was so tough and unyielding that she had a friend with a rototiller turn over the dirt to make it easier for her to work. Once the soil was churned, Leslie was easily able to rake and pick out the grass and weeds that had been growing in the area.

After the ground was rototilled in early May, Leslie checked with me and several other neighbors and friends. This is really one of the best ways to start a perennial garden. You can see what grows well in similar climatic conditions, and you are generally rewarded for your interest with donations of surplus plants. I gave Leslie seedlings or offshoots of bishop's hat, feverfew, phlox, rose campion, rose mallow, sedum, and sundrops. Another neighbor, Jean Woodward, gave her clumps of daylily and black-eyed Susan roots. A friend, Alexandra Radbil, provided columbines, gooseneck plant, and peonies.

Leslie spent one or two afternoons putting these plants in the ground and then decided to add a brick border to the garden. All that work resulted in a rather bare-looking creation. That's where annuals come in. These flowers— many already in full bloom—can be bought at local garden centers and provide instant color and fillers in a new garden. Leslie went out and bought flats of salvia, petunias, and marigolds. These are all inexpensive and provide cheery color in the garden.

The first summer, May. Perennial gardens are not born in a blaze of glory. Pictured here is the garden of Leslie Peirce at its creation. Leslie had spent two afternoons putting in many different kinds of plants and was rewarded with a rather drab result.

△

The first summer, August. Leslie did not despair. She went out and bought several flats of colorful annuals. The red salvia and orange marigolds complemented the color provided by the black-eyed Susans. Note how the foliage from the initial perennial planting has filled out.

◁

The second summer, August. One year later, the perennials in Leslie's garden have begun to shine. The rose mallows were moved to the rear so that their pink flowers and dark green leaves would provide a lush backdrop for the rose campions and black-eyed Susans. Annuals, such as cleome or spider plant, are still part of the garden but their importance has diminished.

The third summer, May. In just two years, Leslie's flower bed has begun to assume the richness of a true perennial garden. Contrast this picture with the one on page 113. While the appearance has improved dramatically, the amount of effort has plummeted. Leslie was completing her Ph.D. dissertation the spring this picture was taken and the only time she had for the garden was to look at it through her window. Since she had skimped on her spring cleaning, however, the garden did require a good three or four hours of weeding in June.

NOW THE GOOD NEWS: THINGS DO GET BETTER

There are two essential characteristics that a gardener with perennials must possess: patience and pride. Patience that the plants will eventually grow and mature, and pride in the progress of each individual one.

Leslie knew that the perennials in her garden would spread in two or three years; at times, that first summer, she did wish they would speed up the process a little. Nevertheless, she enjoyed watching the initial blooms of the first season and becoming more familiar with their appearance and characteristics. And while not essential, Leslie also possesses another trait usually found in gardeners: an inability to resist trying new plants. Throughout that first summer, and in every subsequent one, Leslie has continued to add to her garden through gifts from friends and selected purchases.

In the middle of the garden's second year, Leslie had reached the point where she started to change the placement of plants. This is a natural step in the evolution of a garden. Generally, height is a major consideration in making these shifts. Leslie, for example, found it hard to believe that the tiny rose mallow seedlings I had given her would eventually reach 6 feet. She had placed them in the middle of the flower bed the first year. The following spring, they were all moved to the back.

In addition, it is extremely hard to visualize the correct placement of a plant that grows from 1 to 3 feet tall. You have to see how it eventually performs in your garden, especially in relation to the other flowers you have. If it only gets a little over 1 foot tall, you will probably want it closer to the front; if 3 feet, it will probably be in the middle, if not the back.

Now that Leslie's garden has entered its third year, another common factor has come into play: the combination of new and spreading plants leads to the decision to expand the size of the garden. The process starts all over again.

Both Leslie and I have also enjoyed another aspect of growing many of the easy care perennials in this book. Because they spread rather quickly and must eventually be thinned out, they are great candidates for trades with other gardeners. Leslie and I are fortunate in living in a neighborhood where several people like to garden. We are all constantly trading new plant finds and expanding each other's gardening knowledge. Gardening is seldom a lonely activity.

The last picture, taken two years after the first, shows how Leslie's garden has matured and flourished in a relatively short time period. What was bare space is now filled with good-looking and easy care perennials.

To help give you some ideas on getting your garden started, the following pages present some suggested approaches for three gardens, each having a different light requirement.

COOL ELEGANCE: A SHADE GARDEN

When I first started gardening, I believed shade gardens were the most boring of all. Since they had few flowers, I reasoned that they could be of no possible interest. I have since come to realize that these gardens are perhaps the most challenging to design and, in some ways, the most rewarding when successful.

Foliage form and texture is the key to an elegant shade garden. It allows you to contrast different shapes and sizes in a basically monochromatic scheme. The results are quite lovely and understated.

The shade garden does have its moment of colorful glory in early spring, when sunlight still intrudes. First comes the crystal white snowdrop, closely followed by the rich purple crocus. After that the garden is filled with the intense blue of the Siberian squill and the bold white and yellow of the 'Ice Follies' daffodil. By May, tree leaves are unfolding daily and most of the colors are subdued: the light pinks of bleeding heart and Spanish squill, and the muted blues found in Jacob's ladder and bugloss. Only the boldness of the yellow flag iris really stands out.

By summer, the bulk of the garden design consists of foliage displays. There are the tall, arching leaves of the yellow flag iris; the large, thick, heart-shaped leaves of the bugloss; the undulating green and white leaves of the hosta; the silver-green fernlike foliage of the bleeding heart; and more. These and other easy care perennials in the chart make wonderful design combinations.

You can put large clumps of one kind together and small accent groupings of others. Or, you can have equal numbers of all plants. The choice is yours, and the options—even with this relatively small list of plants—are many.

Don't forget that the hosta will send forth long stems with light blue flowers in midsummer and, if given enough moisture, the bleeding heart will produce sporadic pink blossoms. Toward the end of the summer, the sensitive fern will contribute its dark brown "bead sticks." This activity ensures that your shade garden does not remain static but evolves slowly through the gardening year, in keeping with its cool demeanor.

If you find, nevertheless, that there's just too much green for your taste, don't hesitate to add shade-flowering annuals such as impatiens and begonias. These come in a wide range of colors and will brighten up any dark corner or setting.

PLANTS FOR A SHADE GARDEN, BY SEASON

All these plants will grow in areas that receive from one to three hours of sun per day. While those blooming in early spring require more sunlight, this chart assumes these flowers are growing in areas that are not shaded until tree leaves come out in May.

	EARLY SPRING	LATE SPRING	SUMMER	FALL
FLOWERS	Bishop's hat Bleeding heart Bugloss Crocus Daffodil Grape hyacinth Jacob's ladder Siberian squill Snowdrop Virginia bluebell	Bleeding heart Bugloss Foxglove Iris Jacob's ladder Spanish squill	Astilbe Bleeding heart* Hosta	Bleeding heart*
FOLIAGE		Astilbe Bishop's hat Fern Hosta	Bishop's hat Bugloss Fern Iris Jacob's ladder	Astilbe Bishop's hat Bugloss Fern Hosta Iris Jacob's ladder

* Intermittent bloom

With easy care perennials, a shade garden need not be a problem. The three spring plants shown here, all grown in an area that receives less than three hours of dappled sun, are a good illustration of contrasts in foliage form. The tall, graceful leaves of the yellow flag iris arch over the warm green sensitive fern and the variegated hosta. In summer, these shade greens are enlivened by the light blue flowers of the hosta. In the fall, rich brown, knobby "bead sticks" will shoot up among the sensitive fern; these adorn the garden through winter snows.

GORGEOUS VARIETY: A SEMI-SHADED GARDEN

A semi-shaded garden gives you a bit, if not the best, of both worlds: It allows you the opportunity to grow handsome foliage plants as well as colorful flowers. Many of the plants in this chart—including mountain bluet, aster frikartii, and black-eyed Susan—are more colorful in full sun but will produce some flowers in semi-shade. Others, such as the peony, might not bloom at all with less than four hours of sun but will provide attractive foliage accents. And still others, such as the astilbe and bleeding heart, do best in this kind of setting.

Your main difficulty in starting a semi-shaded garden will be trying to limit the number of plants you purchase. If you want many months of bloom, you must pick from each seasonal category. Some flowers, such as feverfew, bloom throughout two or more seasons and are especially valuable for that reason.

Once you have chosen by time of bloom, you then have to group your plants by height. Short ones, such as candytuft, always go in front. It is probably safe to assume that the rose mallow—which can grow to 6 feet—will be located in the back. You will need a medium-size plant in between the two.

Color becomes an important consideration because there is such an abundance of it. While this is truly a matter of personal taste, it is probably best not to have plants with clashing colors next to each other. Fortunately, you have silver foliage plants—particularly the silver king—and white-flowered ones such as feverfew and gooseneck plant to break up any possible color arguments. Thus, if you wanted to have the red bee balm, the magenta rose campion, and the pink rose mallow together, you just might be able to get away with it if you have generous intermediaries consisting of silver foliage and white flowers.

So there you have it: time, height, and color. Consider each when deciding where to place the wealth of easy care plants that are available.

PLANTS FOR A SEMI-SHADED GARDEN, BY SEASON

All these plants will grow and most will flower in areas that receive from three to seven hours of sun per day. Peonies, for example, will probably not bloom if they only receive three hours of sun per day but will give you handsome foliage.

	EARLY SPRING	LATE SPRING	SUMMER	FALL
FLOWERS	Bishop's hat	Bellflower	Aster frikartii	Anemone
	Bleeding heart	Bleeding heart	Astilbe	Aster frikartii
	Bugloss	Bugloss	Balloon flower	Bee balm*
	Crocus	Candytuft	Bee balm	Black-eyed
	Daffodil	Chives	Bellflower	Susan
	Grape hyacinth	Coral bells	Black-eyed Susan	Bleeding heart*
	Jacob's ladder	Foxglove	Bleeding heart*	Boltonia
	Siberian squill	Iris	Butterfly weed	Chives*
	Snowdrop	Jacob's ladder	Chives*	Feverfew
	Virginia bluebell	Mountain bluet	Coral bells	Mountain bluet*
		Peony	Coreopsis	New York aster
		Phlox	Daylily	Obedient plant
		Spanish squill	Feverfew	Perennial
		Spiderwort	Gooseneck plant	ageratum
		Sundrops	Hosta	Rose mallow*
			Lamb's ears	Sedum
			Lythrum	Spiderwort
			Mountain bluet	Stokesia*
			Perennial ageratum	Yarrow*
			Purple coneflower	
			Rose campion	
			Rose mallow	
			Stokesia	
			Sundrops	
			Tiger lily	
			Yarrow	
FOLIAGE		Astilbe	Anemone	Astilbe
		Bishop's hat	Bishop's hat	Bishop's hat
		Fern	Bugloss	Bugloss
		Hosta	Candytuft	Butterfly weed
		Lamb's ears	Fern	Candytuft
		Rose campion	Iris	Coral bells
		Rose mallow	Jacob's ladder	Daylily
		Sedum	New York aster	Fern
		Silver king	Peony	Hosta
			Sedum	Iris
			Silver king	Jacob's ladder
				Lamb's ears
				Peony
				Rose campion
				Silver king
				Sundrops

* Intermittent bloom

A wealth of plants and color combinations are available for a garden in semi-shade, defined as one that receives from three to seven hours of sun a day. These two pages show how just changing one plant in a grouping can lead to quite different effects. In the picture on the left, the gray leaves and magenta flowers of the rose campion are combined with blue spiderworts and yellow sun drops. The latter two flowers are also featured in the picture on the right. However, the substitution of the white "Deutschland" astilbe for the rose campion produces a much different mood.

HOT COLORS: A FULL-SUN GARDEN

Sunshine seems to vitalize a flower, almost making it want to be as colorful and as lush as the rays pouring down upon it. Sun gardens are magnificent tapestries of color and rich green foliage. They do, however, have their special requirements. To paraphrase a wonderful line by Hugh Johnson: in Gauguin settings, it takes forty horse pigmentation to register any color at all. Sun gardens require a minimum of two or three really bold colors, the kind of yellows found in black-eyed Susans or of oranges in tiger lilies.

It's fun to experiment with color themes throughout the garden year, and this can easily be accomplished with a sun garden, where the overall palette can vary dramatically from month to month.

In early spring, for example, the motif could be blue and white, with an ever-so-soft undercurrent of light yellow. This would feature white snowdrops and rich blue Siberian squill, followed by "Ice Follies" daffodils where the yellow slowly fades to warm white and then the bugloss with its warm blue flowers.

By late spring, when the sun has yet to reach full-force glare, the whole garden could shift to muted tones of blue, a hint of pink, and strong white. This would feature flowers such as candytuft, chives, foxglove, peony, Spanish squill, mountain bluet, and bellflower.

Bold oranges and yellows could then march to the fore to meet the brilliant summer sun. Flowers that would rise to such a challenge include black-eyed Susans, butterfly weed, coreopsis, daylily, tiger lily, and the indispensable feverfew as a white buffer among the various groups.

In the fall, the color scheme could once again settle down and encourage pinks. Anemone, obedient plant, and sedum all bloom this time of year and could look handsome next to the flowers of the black-eyed Susan and feverfew.

This scheme not only gives you a dramatic change in viewing pleasure but also provides an abundance of cut flowers to take indoors for arrangements.

PLANTS FOR A SUN GARDEN, BY SEASON

All these plants will grow in areas that receive eight or more hours of sun per day.

	EARLY SPRING	LATE SPRING	SUMMER	FALL

FLOWERS	Bugloss
	Crocus
	Daffodil
	Grape hyacinth
	Siberian squill
	Snowdrop
		Bellflower
		Bugloss
		Candytuft
		Chives
		Coral bells
		Foxglove
		Iris
		Mountain bluet
		Peony
		Spanish squill
		Spiderwort
		Sundrops
			Aster frikartii
			Balloon flower
			Bee balm
			Bellflower
			Black-eyed
			  Susan
			Butterfly weed
			Chives*
			Coral bells
			Coreopsis
			Daylily
			Feverfew
			Gooseneck plant
			Lamb's ears
			Lythrum
			Mountain bluet
			Perennial
			  ageratum
			Purple
			  coneflower
			Rose campion
			Rose mallow
			Stokesia
			Sundrops
			Tiger lily
			Yarrow
				Anemone
				Aster frikartii
				Bee balm*
				Black-eyed
				  Susan
				Boltonia
				Chives*
				Feverfew
				Mountain bluet*
				New York aster
				Obedient plant
				Perennial
				  ageratum
				Rose mallow*
				Sedum
				Spiderwort
				Stokesia*
				Yarrow*

FOLIAGE		Fern Lamb's ears Sedum Silver king	Anemone Bugloss Candytuft Fern Iris New York aster Peony Sedum Silver king	Bugloss Butterfly weed Candytuft Coral bells Daylily Fern Iris Lamb's ears Peony Rose campion Silver king Sundrops

* Intermittent bloom

A bold orange, such as that provided by the butterfly weed, is perfect for the summer garden in full sun. This flower and two other orange perennials—tiger lilies and daylilies—can go for long periods without being watered.

The plant pictured here grows in the garden of my neighbor, Jean Woodward. Jean loves fiery colors and supplements her perennial plantings with many bright annuals, including marigolds and zinnias. The large leaves of the plant flanking the butterfly weed belong to one of her favorites, the annual Mexican sunflower or tithonia.

While this book highlights perennials, it is not meant to disdain annuals. Many of these colorful flowers are particularly suited to sun gardens and are excellent for covering up bare spots left by spring-flowering bulbs.

CHORES: THEY'RE MINIMAL BUT ESSENTIAL

All of the above garden designs utilize the easy care perennials discussed in this book. There are, however, certain tasks that you must not neglect if you want the garden to remain a low-maintenance one.

First, a good house cleaning is essential. This means all weeds must go. It's a task that need be done only twice a year: in the spring when you rake the beds, and in the fall before the first deluge of leaves. Weeds are not only unsightly but also harbor many diseases and insect pests.

Second, mulch the garden in early summer. To mulch is to cover the ground around the plants with grass clippings or peat moss or any other material offered at your local garden center. Grass clippings are probably the cheapest approach. The mulch—a garden blanket, really —keeps moisture from evaporating and smothers many potential weeds. As the mulch eventually breaks down, it forms organic matter that can enrich your soil.

Third, water when the plants start to look droopy. If they get dry and worn out, they could become susceptible to disease and infection. Usually, spring rains do your watering chores for you in the early part of the garden year. When summer heat strikes, however, you should pay closer attention to your plants. If your soil is blanketed with mulch, you will probably need to give your flowers a good soaking only once a week. Since many of these plants can go for long periods without watering, don't worry if you are away for a two- or three-week vacation. The flowers may be desperately parched upon your return, but if you water immediately, most will probably survive—albeit a bit grumpily at first.

Fourth, watch out for sick plants. You have to practice a "survival of the fittest" ethic. If a plant is not doing well—especially after a good watering—it has to go so that it won't have a chance to harm others. Just cut the foliage to the ground, put the refuse in a plastic bag to trap fungi or insects, and dispose of it. If a perennial looks sick right down to its roots, I dig up the entire plant and throw it away.

Some plants can survive attacks. For example, I let the Japanese beetles have a go at my sundrops because the plants do not seem so harmed as to not flower next year. In other cases, most notably infestations of the four-lined plant bug, I shake rotenone dust over the plants two or three times during the summer, and that seems to keep things under control. In general, however, it is best to dispose of sick or infected plants to make sure the garden stays an easy care one.

Five, stake where necessary. You really don't have to do this, but the garden does get a bit messy looking and you lose lots of the flavor of the flowers when they are flat on their backs. You can buy stakes and garden string at your local garden center. It takes about two to three minutes per plant to accomplish this easy and painless job.

Discussions involving disease and garden stakes somehow miss out on conveying the pleasure of gardening. Never lose sight of the big picture—a lovely flower bed. This leads to the last, but perhaps most essential point of this book.

AN IMPORTANT REMINDER: HAVE A GOOD TIME

Growing flowers is perhaps the most elusive and fragile form of creative activity. The result is never permanent, always changing with each shift in light and weather patterns. While this means the joys are fleeting, so too are the mistakes.

There's a peaceful side to gardening. After a long, busy day dealing with cranky customers, challenging problems, or tired children, you'll find that the garden welcomes you with a quiet beauty. It provides serenity and fragrance, a reminder of the immensity of our planet and how we are all part of it and yet so uniquely individual.

Easy care gardening provides an added bonus. It's fun. It is not and should not be serious gardening. With the perennials described in this book, you can produce a work of art with only minimal effort.

What's more, your garden will be an interesting one, an ever-changing kaleidoscope of color throughout the growing season. Unlike a relatively static annual flower garden, your easy care perennial plants will shoot up, flower, and disappear—only to be quickly replaced by another lovely scene. These flowers will be a visual symphony of color, loud at some times, soft at others, always something to take pride in. Your easy care garden will be your very own creation. Be proud of it and enjoy it!

APPENDIX

PLANT
SOURCES

Without question, the easiest, most convenient, and cheapest way to obtain plants is as gifts from neighbors. Pictured here is the garden of Mickey Eggers, located just four houses down from mine. Mickey—only her husband calls her Margaret— has a handsome garden that glories in bold summer colors. Offshoots from the purple coneflowers, gooseneck plants, and daylilies blooming here are now flourishing in my flower beds. In turn, I have given Mickey columbines, foxgloves, feverfew, sundrops, and perennial ageratum.

There are four basic ways to obtain plants: (1) as gifts from the gardens of friends or neighbors; (2) as purchases from local garden centers; (3) as seedlings that you've raised yourself; and (4) as orders through the mail from nurseries.

As mentioned earlier in this book, the cheapest and simplest way to obtain plants is through donations from friends and neighbors. Friends can tell you how plants behave in their gardens and neighbors can give you specific growing tips for your area of the country. These "friendship flowers" add a warm, personal dimension to a garden. As I walk about and look at many of my colorful flowers, I see mementos of trips around the country and remember gardening conversations with many treasured friends.

If you don't have the wealth of gardening friends that I am blessed with, your next best bet is to obtain your plants from a garden center rather than through the mail. Though the cost for local purchases may be higher, this is still the more efficient way to stock your garden. When you go to your local store, you can inspect plants closely and make sure they are in good condition. In addition, you can choose the exact day you want to work in your garden; mail-order perennials sometimes arrive at inconvenient planting times.

Not all garden centers are alike, however. Make sure the one you buy from has knowledgeable personnel: people who know the botanical names of plants, who can give you helpful growing advice, and who can make suggestions for the most suitable plants in your area. Notice how the plants are cared for. They should have some protection from hot sun and never be allowed to dry out.

The best local garden centers—from your point of view—are the kinds that are nurseries in their own right. These operations raise most of their own plants. You can visit their growing fields and see exactly what a particular plant looks like and how it performs. Weston Nurseries in Hopkinton, Massachusetts, is a good example of this kind of business. Its garden center is surrounded by 800 acres of nursery—beautiful fields filled with an incredible array of plants. Professional horticulturists are on hand to answer any questions you may have. If you live near such a place, you are in good gardening hands.

Many of the perennials in this book can be obtained from either of the above two sources, and you are best advised to start with them if possible. Other flowers, however, are easy to grow but difficult to locate. If these plants should prove appealing to you, you will probably have to order them through the mail from a seed firm or a nursery.

SEED FIRMS

The following three firms are among the largest in the industry. When you browse through their catalogues, you will see a variety of offerings that garden centers simply cannot match. If you are the kind of person who gets stricken with acute garden fever in the bleak depths of February, you might want to order packets of easy care perennial seeds from one of these firms and raise your own seedlings.

HARRIS SEEDS

961 LYELL AVENUE
ROCHESTER, NEW YORK
14606

Harris has been in business since 1879 and is particularly well known in the Northeast and Midwest for the quality and productivity of its seeds. These come well-packaged and with good growing instructions. Harris pays for all shipping charges, and supplies refunds upon request and with the return of empty seed packets. When an ordered item is out of stock, Harris automatically substitutes unless you check the "No Substitutions" box on the order form. There is no minimum purchase requirement. Harris does not list any phone number.

EASY CARE PERENNIAL SEEDS

BOTANICAL NAME	POPULAR NAME
ACHILLEA MILLEFOLIUM	YARROW
ALLIUM SCHOENOPRASUM	CHIVES
ASCLEPIAS TUBEROSA	BUTTERFLY WEED
COREOPSIS LANCEOLATA	COREOPSIS
ECHINACEA PURPUREA	PURPLE CONEFLOWER
IBERIS SEMPERVIRENS	CANDYTUFT
PHYSOSTEGIA VIRGINIANA	OBEDIENT PLANT
STACHYS BYZANTINA*	LAMB'S EARS

* Listed as *Stachys lanata*

PARK SEED
COMPANY

COKESBURY ROAD
GREENWOOD,
SOUTH CAROLINA

29647-0001
(803) 223-7333

Founded in 1868 by George W. Park, this is the oldest and largest family-owned seed company in the United States. The company features extensive trial gardens that attract visitors from all over the world. Customers may write or call for horticultural advice. Seeds are well packaged with clear growing instructions. If you are not completely satisfied with your order, Park will refund your money or replace the order; you have one year to voice your complaint. Shipping charges are paid by the company, though they do have a negligible handling charge. There are no minimum purchase requirements, and you can indicate on the order form whether or not you will accept substitutes.

EASY CARE PERENNIAL SEEDS

BOTANICAL NAME	POPULAR NAME
ALLIUM SCHOENOPRASUM	CHIVES
ASCLEPIAS TUBEROSA	BUTTERFLY WEED
ASTILBE X ARENDSII	ASTILBE
CROCUS VERNUS "DUTCH CROCUS"	CROCUS
DIGITALIS PURPUREA	FOXGLOVE
GALANTHUS NIVALIS	SNOWDROPS
IBERIS SEMPERVIRENS	CANDYTUFT
MALVA ALCEA "FASTIGIATA"	ROSE MALLOW
NARCISSUS "ICE FOLLIES"	DAFFODIL
PLATYCODON GRANDIFLORUS	BALLOON FLOWER
RUDBECKIA FULGIDA "GOLDSTURM"	BLACK-EYED SUSAN

THOMPSON &
MORGAN

P. O. BOX 1308
JACKSON, NEW JERSEY
08527

(201) 363-2225

This British company was established in 1855 and is renowned in gardening circles for the tremendous variety of flower and vegetable seed that it offers. In some cases, Thompson & Morgan is the only known seed source for rare or endangered species. You are asked to list acceptable substitutes on the order form; if you don't, the firm will send something of their own choosing if they are out of stock for the items you have requested. If you don't care for this policy, state so on your order and request either a refund or a credit. Thompson & Morgan guarantees to replace seeds should there be reasonable cause for complaint; a time limit for such cause is not given. Given their care in packaging and their precise growing instructions, they probably feel valid complaints should be rare. There is no minimum purchase requirement. While the company pays all shipping costs, there is a very small, flat handling charge.

EASY CARE PERENNIAL SEEDS

BOTANICAL NAME	POPULAR NAME
ALLIUM SCHOENOPRASUM	CHIVES
AQUILEGIA VULGARIS	COLUMBINE
ASCLEPIAS TUBEROSA	BUTTERFLY WEED
ASTER X FRIKARTII "WONDER OF STAFFA"	ASTER FRIKARTII
CAMPANULA PERSICIFOLIA "TELHAM BEAUTY"	BELLFLOWER
CENTAUREA MONTANA	MOUNTAIN BLUET
CHRYSANTHEMUM PARTHENIUM*	FEVERFEW
DICENTRA EXIMIA	BLEEDING HEART
DIGITALIS PURPUREA	FOXGLOVE
LYSIMACHIA CLETHROIDES	GOOSENECK PLANT
MALVA ALCEA "FASTIGIATA"	ROSE MALLOW
MERTENSIA VIRGINICA	VIRGINIA BLUEBELL
PHLOX DIVARICATA	PHLOX
PHYSOSTEGIA VIRGINIANA	OBEDIENT PLANT
RUDBECKIA FULGIDA "GOLDSTURM"	BLACK-EYED SUSAN
STACHYS BYZANTINA**	LAMB'S EARS

* Listed under Herbs as "Parthenium Matricaria"
** Listed as *Stachys lanata*

MAIL-ORDER NURSERIES

Mail-order nurseries come in all sizes and shapes. Some are huge operations; J. W. Jung, for example, sends out over 1 million catalogues a year. Others, such as Native Gardens, are small, family-owned businesses that specialize in certain plants. The nurseries in this book were chosen to represent this diversity. Geography played a role, too: the firms are located throughout the United States, in the North, South, East, and West.

It's important to recognize that there is no one best nursery. Each has its own distinctive personality, as well as its particular strengths and weaknesses. You are well advised to be on the mailing list for at least two of these firms. That way, you can comparison shop as well as read about new plants. Most nurseries try to specialize, to sell plants not available elsewhere. It's fun to read about these perennials in mail-order catalogues during the winter.

One of the firms you order from should probably be chosen on the basis of location; that is, nearness to your garden. Nurseries on the Pacific Coast, for example, offer plants raised on site and probably best adapted to that growing region. On the other hand, it's fun to examine the offerings of firms far away from your home because you might discover an easy care plant that is not popular in your area but that would nevertheless thrive in your garden.

The primary *raison d'etre* for all these businesses is to sell plants. If they have dissatisfied customers, they cannot stay in business. Each tries to offer a special service—ranging from choice of plants, to low prices, to refund policy —that will distinguish it from others. These services are all touched upon in the descriptions of each nursery that follows. I feel that some nurseries clearly stand out in certain areas, and these subjective evaluations follow:

Best written catalogue: Holbrook Farm and Nursery, White Flower Farm
Best illustrated catalogue: Wayside Gardens, White Flower Farm
Best prices: Bluestone Perennials, J. W. Jung
Best refund policy: Bluestone Perennials, Wayside
Most easy care offerings: Carroll Gardens, Milaeger's Gardens, White Flower Farm
Most personable service: Holbrook Farm and Nursery
Best substitution policy: Crownsville Nursery, McClure & Zimmerman

Mail-order nurseries are not static operations. They are constantly adding and deleting plants from their lists. I personally talked with representatives—and, in the case of the smaller nurseries, with the owners—of the sixteen nurseries described below. All have assured me that they will offer the plants under their listing in this appendix at least through 1989. If there is sufficient demand—and these people are, after all, profit-making concerns—the plants will probably continue to be offered. In addition, several may add other plants described in this book.

Often a nursery will run out of an item and send a substitute. Personally, I dislike this practice. I once received a fuschia when I had ordered a geranium, and even though the former was more expensive and sent at no extra charge, it was not what I wanted. Therefore, in each nursery description that follows, I have indicated if you need to state whether you will accept a substitute.

Refunds, shipping charges, and minimum purchase requirements are all important considerations. These are also covered under each nursery description.

BLUESTONE
PERENNIALS

7211 MIDDLE RIDGE ROAD
MADISON, OHIO 44057
(800) 852-5243
(January through June,
8 AM to 8 PM)
(216) 428-7535

Bluestone Perennials is a wholesale supplier to garden centers across the country. The firm's plants are grown in little plastic containers—the very same six-packs you buy locally. You can now purchase these direct at just about wholesale prices. In most cases, Bluestone's prices are at least half those of the other nurseries on this list. The seedlings you receive are small, but they are well packaged and have markers for identification. Some of the plants will bloom the first year; most, because of size, take two years.

Bluestone has a very liberal refund offer: if you have a complaint, they will reship the plant or return your money; there is no time limit on this policy. You may order as much or as little as you like, and the shipping charges are quite low. You can call for plant information and horticultural advice. Probably because of the huge scale of their operations, Bluestone does not expect to be out of stock and does not substitute on orders.

EASY CARE PERENNIAL OFFERINGS

BOTANICAL NAME	POPULAR NAME
ALLIUM SCHOENOPRASUM	CHIVES
ANEMONE VITIFOLIA "ROBUSTISSIMA"	ANEMONE
ARTEMISIA LUDOVICIANA VAR. ALBULA 'SILVER KING'	SILVER KING
ASTER X FRIKARTII "WONDER OF STAFFA"	ASTER FRIKARTII
ASTILBE X ARENDSII*	ASTILBE
BOLTONIA ASTEROIDES "SNOWBANK"	BOLTONIA
CAMPANULA PESICIFOLIA	BELLFLOWER
CENTAUREA MONTANA	MOUNTAIN BLUET
ECHINACEA PURPUREA	PURPLE CONEFLOWER
LYSIMACHIA CLETHROIDES	GOOSENECK PLANT
MALVA ALCEA "FASTIGIATA"	ROSE MALLOW
OENOTHERA FRUTICOSA**	SUNDROPS
PLATYCODON GRANDIFLORUS†	BALLOON FLOWER
RUDBECKIA FULGIDA "GOLDSTURM"	BLACK-EYED SUSAN
STACHYS BYZANTINA‡	LAMB'S EARS

* **Not identified as** *arendsii*
** **Listed as** *Oenothera youngi*
† Listed as *Platycodon grandiflorum*
‡ Listed as *Stachys lanata*

W. ATLEE BURPEE
& COMPANY

300 PARK AVENUE
WARMINSTER,
PENNSYLVANIA 18974
(215) 674-4915

Burpee is one of the largest sellers of packaged seeds in the United States. In 1987, sales were flat and this contributed to a reconsideration of strategy. The firm's limited offerings of perennial plants were doing quite well, in line with national trends. Burpee decided to initiate a dramatic shift in its method of doing business. The number of perennial plant offerings was increased by a factor of 10; and a separate catalogue, first distributed in fall 1988, was published for these plants. The Burpee people also decided to grow their stock vegetatively; that is, from root cuttings and tissue culture rather than from seed. This allows guaranteed uniformity in plant appearance and gives Burpee the opportunity to offer a wide range of cultivars, which do not come true from seed and which the Burpee officials feel are superior to species plants in most cases.

Burpee prides itself on the quality of its service. The plants arrive well packaged and the growing information is quite helpful. Burpee pays all shipping charges and has a modest handling charge. You may order as much or as little as you like, and there is a customer service number to review any questions. Be sure to mark "no substitutes" on the order form.

EASY CARE PERENNIAL OFFERINGS

BOTANICAL NAME	POPULAR NAME
ALLIUM SCHOENOPRASUM	CHIVES
ARTEMISIA LUDOVICIANA VAR. ALBULA "SILVER KING"	SILVER KING
ASCLEPIAS TUBEROSA	BUTTERFLY WEED
ASTER X FRIKARTII "WONDER OF STAFFA"	ASTER FRIKARTII
ASTER NOVI-BELGII	NEW YORK ASTER
BOLTONIA ASTEROIDES "SNOWBANK"	BOLTONIA
BRUNNERA MACROPHYLLA	BUGLOSS
CROCUS VERNUS "DUTCH CROCUS"	CROCUS
DIGITALIS PURPUREA	FOXGLOVE
GALANTHUS NIVALIS	SNOWDROPS
HOSTA UNDULATA	HOSTA
IBERIS SEMPERVIRENS	CANDYTUFT
LYTHRUM SALICARIA "MORDEN PINK"	LYTHRUM
MERTENSIA VIRGINICA	VIRGINIA BLUEBELL
MUSCARI BOTRYOIDES	GRAPE HYACINTH
NARCISSUS "ICE FOLLIES"	DAFFODIL
PAEONIA LACTIFLORA "FESTIVA MAXIMA"	PEONY
RUDBECKIA FULGIDA "GOLDSTURM"	BLACK-EYED SUSAN
SCILLA SIBERICA	SIBERIAN SQUILL
STOKESIA LAEVIS	STOKESIA, CORNFLOWER

BUSSE GARDENS

ROUTE 2, BOX 238
COKATO,
MINNESOTA 55321
(612) 286-2654

This is a family-owned business—the Busse Bunch, as they like to call themselves—that was started in 1977. The Busses have lovely display beds and encourage visitors to see the plants. They specialize in daylilies, hostas, irises, and peonies. Their catalogue is quite helpful in that it includes the names and addresses of the societies specializing in these plants. If you do not want substitutions for out-of-stock items, you must indicate this on your order form. Refunds are given only if you claim them within five days of receiving your order. There is a minimum purchase requirement and shipping charges that are about average. I have a special fondness for this nursery because they are one of the few general perennial ones in the country offering one of my favorite plants, the yellow flag iris.

EASY CARE PERENNIAL OFFERINGS

BOTANICAL NAME	PLANT NAME
ANEMONE VITIFOLIA "ROBUSTISSIMA"	ANEMONE
ASCLEPIAS TUBEROSA	BUTTERFLY WEED
ASTER NOVI-BELGII	NEW YORK ASTER
ASTILBE X ARENDSII	ASTILBE
BRUNNERA MACROPHYLLA	BUGLOSS
DICENTRA EXIMIA	BLEEDING HEART
HEMEROCALLIS FULVA	DAYLILY
HEUCHERA SANGUINEA	CORAL BELLS
HOSTA UNDULATA*	HOSTA
IRIS PSEUDACORUS	IRIS
MERTENSIA VIRGINICA	VIRGINIA BLUEBELL
ONOCLEA SENSIBILIS	FERNS
PAEONIA LACTIFLORA "FESTIVA MAXIMA"	PEONY
PHLOX DIVARICATA	PHLOX
RUDBECKIA FULGIDA "GOLDSTURM"	BLACK-EYED SUSAN
STACHYS BYZANTIN**	LAMB'S EARS

* Listed as Hosta undulata "Variegated"
** Listed as Stachys lanata

CARROLL
GARDENS

444 EAST MAIN STREET
P.O. BOX 310
WESTMINSTER, MARYLAND
21157
(800) 638-6334
(outside Maryland)
(301) 848-5422

Few nurseries can match the variety of perennials offered by Carroll Gardens. This large mail-order firm ships to all states, except Hawaii, and to Canada. The supply of each plant is limited, however, and if you don't want substitutes, be sure to note this on your order form. Then, if your order cannot be filled, you will automatically receive a credit; refunds must be requested. The Carroll Gardens guarantee covers the arrival of plants only; written complaints must be made within ten days of an order's arrival. There is no minimum purchase requirement, except for those paid by credit card. Shipping charges vary with size of the order and average about 12 percent of the total. Carroll Gardens has a large retail operation, where it offers supplies and books in addition to its container-grown plants. These people are particularly helpful about tracking down plants that are hard to find, and welcome inquiries about perennials not listed in their catalogue.

EASY CARE PERENNIAL OFFERINGS

BOTANICAL NAME	PLANT NAME
ALLIUM SCHOENOPRASUM	CHIVES
ANEMONE VITIFOLIA "ROBUSTISSIMA"	ANEMONE
ARTEMISIA LUDOVICIANA VAR. ALBULA 'SILVER KING'	SILVER KING
ASCLEPIAS TUBEROSA	BUTTERFLY WEED
ASTER X FRIKARTII "WONDER OF STAFFA"	ASTER FRIKARTII
ASTER NOVI-BELGII	NEW YORK ASTER
ASTILBE X ARENDSII	ASTILBE
BOLTONIA ASTEROIDES "SNOWBANK"	BOLTONIA
BRUNNERA MACROPHYLLA*	BUGLOSS
CAMPANULA PERSICIFOLIA**	BELLFLOWER
CENTAUREA MONTANA	MOUNTAIN BLUET
CHRYSANTHEMUM PARTHENIUM	FEVERFEW
COREOPSIS LANCEOLATA	COREOPSIS
DICENTRA EXIMIA	BLEEDING HEART

* Listed as *Anchusa myosotidiflora*
** Listed as *Campanula persicifolia caerulea*

(cont.)

BOTANICAL NAME	PLANT NAME
DIGITALIS PURPUREA	FOXGLOVE
ECHINACEA PURPUREA	PURPLE CONEFLOWER
EPIMEDIUM GRANDIFLORUM	BISHOP'S HAT
EUPATORIUM COELESTINUM	PERENNIAL AGERATUM
HEMEROCALLIS FULVA†	DAYLILY
HOSTA UNDULATA	HOSTA
IBERIS SEMPERVIRENS	CANDYTUFT
IRIS PSEUDACORUS†	IRIS
LYCHNIS CORONARIA	ROSE CAMPION
LYSIMACHIA CLETHROIDES	GOOSENECK PLANT
LYTHRUM SALICARIA "MORDEN PINK"	LYTHRUM
MALVA ALCEA "FASTIGIATA"	ROSE MALLOW
MERTENSIA VIRGINICA	VIRGINIA BLUEBELL
OENOTHERA FRUTICOSA‡	SUNDROPS
ONOCLEA SENSIBILIS	FERNS
PAEONIA LACTIFLORA "FESTIVA MAXIMA"	PEONY
PLATYCODON GRANDIFLORUS	BALLOON FLOWER
POLEMONIUM REPTANS	JACOB'S LADDER
RUDBECKIA FULGIDA "GOLDSTURM"	BLACK-EYED SUSAN
TRADESCANTIA X ANDERSONIA "BLUE STONE"	SPIDERWORT

† Special request order; not listed in catalogue.
‡ Listed as *Oenothera tetragona*

THE
CROWNSVILLE
NURSERY

P.O. BOX 797
CROWNSVILLE,
MARYLAND 21032
(301) 923-2212

The Crownsville Nursery offers a wide variety of perennials at very reasonable prices. The firm has both mail-order and retail operations. The retail plants are normally larger and more expensive than those sold by mail. Just about all mail-order plants are grown in 3½-inch pots that have over-wintered outdoors. Plants are guaranteed to arrive in good condition and if there is a problem, you are urged to contact the firm. Crownsville has a most commendable policy with regard to substitution. If they cannot fill your order, they automatically refund your money. Shipping charges approximate their actual cost and are thus as low as possible. There is no service charge ut there is a $25 minimum purchase requirement.

EASY CARE PERENNIAL OFFERINGS

BOTANICAL NAME	POPULAR NAME
ACHILLEA MILLEFOLIUM	YARROW
ALLIUM SCHOENOPRASUM	CHIVES
AQUILEGIA VULGARIS	COLUMBINE
ARTEMISIA LUDOVICIANA VAR. ALBULA "SILVER KING"	SILVER KING
ASCLEPIAS TUBEROSA	BUTTERFLY WEED
ASTER X FRIKARTII "WONDER OF STAFFA"	ASTER FRIKARTII
ASTILBE X ARENDSII	ASTILBE
BRUNNERA MACROPHYLLA	BUGLOSS
CAMPANULA PERSICIFOLIA	BELLFLOWER
EUPATORIUM COELESTINUM	PERENNIAL AGERATUM
HEMEROCALLIS FULVA	DAYLILY
HOSTA UNDULATA	HOSTA
LYCHNIS CORONARIA	ROSE CAMPION
LYSIMACHIA CLETHROIDES	GOOSENECK PLANT
LYTHRUM SALICARIA "MORDEN PINK"	LYTHRUM
MALVA ALCEA "FASTIGIATA"	ROSE MALLOW
PLATYCODON GRANDIFLORUS	BALLOON FLOWER
POLEMONIUM REPTANS	JACOB'S LADDER
RUDBECKIA FULGIDA "GOLDSTURM"	BLACK-EYED SUSAN
STACHYS BYZANTINA	LAMB'S EARS
STOKESIA LAEVIS	STOKESIA, CORNFLOWER

HOLBROOK FARM
& NURSERY

ROUTE 2, BOX 223B
FLETCHER,
NORTH CAROLINA 28732
(704) 891-7790

You get a real appreciation for southern hospitality and charm when you deal with Holbrook Farm & Nursery, which is owned by Allen W. Bush. His catalogue reads like a personal letter, and a most interesting one at that. He even sends customers postcards throughout the year to tell about new developments. Either he or one of his personable assistants is at the phone to answer questions each afternoon between 5 and 6 PM. Visitors to the nursery are most cordially welcomed (and several find their pictures in his catalogue the following year). When ordering plants, you must indicate your willingness to accept substitutions on the form. If you are not satisfied with your order, you must let the company know within sixty days; they will offer you a choice of replacement, credit, or refund. There is no minimum purchase requirement. While the prices are on the high side, so too is the service.

EASY CARE PERENNIAL OFFERINGS

BOTANICAL NAME	POPULAR NAME
ASCLEPIAS TUBEROSA	BUTTERFLY WEED
ASTILBE X ARENDSII	ASTILBE
BOLTONIA ASTEROIDES "SNOWBANK"	BOLTONIA
BRUNNERA MACROPHYLLA	BUGLOSS
CAMPANULA PERSICIFOLIA*	BELLFLOWER
ECHINACEA PURPUREA	PURPLE CONEFLOWER
EUPATORIUM COELESTINUM	PERENNIAL AGERATUM
LYSIMACHIA CLETHROIDES	GOOSENECK PLANT
LYTHRUM SALICARIA "MORDEN PINK"	LYTHRUM
MALVA ALCEA "FASTIGIATA"	ROSE MALLOW
RUDBECKIA FULGIDA "GOLDSTURM"	BLACK-EYED SUSAN

* Listed as *Campanula persicifolia* 'Grandiflora'

J. W. JUNG
SEED COMPANY

335 SOUTH HIGH STREET
RANDOLPH, WISCONSIN
53957-0001
(414) 326-3121

The Jung family started their company in 1907, and its members have actively participated in it ever since. It is one of the largest in the industry. Though the company is primarily known for the quality of its seed packets, it has recently begun to expand its perennial plant offerings. More are expected to be added to their current listing. Their prices are among the lowest you can find. Jung will replace any plants that do not grow according to instructions; they must be notified within a specified time period (usually several months). There is no minimum purchase requirement and shipping charges are extremely low. Jung does substitute when they run out of particular items, so be sure to mark your preference about this on the order form.

EASY CARE PERENNIAL OFFERINGS

BOTANICAL NAME	POPULAR NAME
ASTILBE X ARENDSII*	ASTILBE
GALANTHUS NIVALIS	SNOWDROPS
HEUCHERA SANGUINEA	CORAL BELLS
HOSTA UNDULATA**	HOSTA
LYTHRUM SALICARIA "MORDEN PINK"†	LYTHRUM
MERTENSIA VIRGINICA	VIRGINIA BLUEBELL
NARCISSUS "ICE FOLLIES"	DAFFODIL
OENOTHERA FRUTICOSA	SUNDROPS
RUDBECKIA FULGIDA "GOLDSTURM"	BLACK-EYED SUSAN

  * Not identified as *arendsii*
 ** Listed as *Hosta variegata*
  † Listed as *Lythrum virgatum*

LAMB
NURSERIES

EAST 101 SHARP AVENUE
SPOKANE, WASHINGTON
99202
(509) 328-7956

Lamb Nurseries offers an interesting collection of perennials, many of them rare and hard to find. Local customers can visit on Fridays and Saturdays. The firm ships to every state; charges vary with the size of the order and range from 15 to 25 percent of the total. There is no minimum purchase requirement. If plants do not arrive in satisfactory condition, you must notify Lamb Nurseries within ten days to get replacements. Supplies on some of the plants are limited; indicate on the order form if you are willing to accept substitutes.

EASY CARE PERENNIAL OFFERINGS

BOTANICAL NAME	POPULAR NAME
ANEMONE VITIFOLIA "ROBUSTISSIMA"	ANEMONE
ARTEMISIA LUDOVICIANA VAR. ALBULA "SILVER KING"	SILVER KING
ASTER X FRIKARTII "WONDER OF STAFFA"	ASTER FRIKARTII
ASTILBE X ARENDSII	ASTILBE
BRUNNERA MACROPHYLLA	BUGLOSS
CENTAUREA MONTANA	MOUNTAIN BLUET
HOSTA UNDULATA*	HOSTA
LYCHNIS CORONARIA	ROSE CAMPION
LYTHRUM SALICARIA "MORDEN PINK"	LYTHRUM
RUDBECKIA FULGIDA "GOLDSTURM"	BLACK-EYED SUSAN

* Listed as *Hosta undulata variegata*

MCCLURE &
ZIMMERMAN

108 WEST WINNEBAGO
P.O. BOX 368
FRIESLAND, WISCONSIN
53935
(414) 326-4220

This company specializes in bulbs and offers a wide variety of imports as well as native kinds. If you have any doubts about the quality of the bulbs received, McClure & Zimmerman will honor your preference for a replacement or a refund. The firm does not substitute, and re-funds money on orders it cannot fill. Shipping charges vary by location and average about 12 percent of an order's total. Prices are higher, but the bulb selection is greater than those posted by nurseries that also sell plants.

EASY CARE PERENNIAL OFFERINGS

BOTANICAL NAME	POPULAR NAME
CROCUS VERNUS "DUTCH CROCUS"	CROCUS
ENDYMION HISPANICUS	SPANISH SQUILL, WOOD HYACINTH
GALANTHUS NIVALIS	SNOWDROPS
MUSCARI BOTRYOIDES	GRAPE HYACINTH
NARCISSUS "ICE FOLLIES"	DAFFODIL
SCILLA SIBERICA	SIBERIAN SQUILL

MILAEGER'S
GARDENS

4838 DOUGLAS AVENUE
RACINE, WISCONSIN
53402-2498

(414) 639-2371

Milaeger's has a large retail operation, where visitors can personally inspect plants they want to buy as well as listen to horticultural lectures and pick up garden supplies, furniture, and accessories. The family has been involved in the business for over forty years. Prices are very competitive, especially considering there are no shipping charges. The firm does specify minimum purchase amounts and claims must be made within fifteen days to be considered; replacement or credit is offered. Plants are large and extremely well packaged. If you indicate you do not want substitutes on the order form and Milaeger's is unable to fill your order, you will be issued a credit.

EASY CARE PERENNIAL OFFERINGS

BOTANICAL NAME	POPULAR NAME
ALLIUM SCHOENOPRASUM	CHIVES
ANEMONE VITIFOLIA "ROBUSTISSIMA"	ANEMONE
ARTEMISIA LUDOVICIANA VAR. ALBULA "SILVER KING"	SILVER KING
ASCLEPIAS TUBEROSA	BUTTERFLY WEED
ASTER X FRIKARTII "WONDER OF STAFFA"	ASTER FRIKARTII
ASTER NOVI-BELGII	NEW YORK ASTER
ASTILBE X ARENDSII	ASTILBE
BOLTONIA ASTEROIDES "SNOWBANK"	BOLTONIA
BRUNNERA MACROPHYLLA	BUGLOSS
CAMPANULA PERSICIFOLIA*	BELLFLOWER
CENTAUREA MONTANA	MOUNTAIN BLUET
CHRYSANTHEMUM PARTHENIUM**	FEVERFEW
ECHINACEA PURPUREA	PURPLE CONEFLOWER
EUPATORIUM COELESTINUM	PERENNIAL AGERATUM
HEUCHERA SANGUINEA	CORAL BELLS
HOSTA ULDULATA†	HOSTA
IBERIS SEMPERVIRENS	CANDYTUFT
LYSIMACHIA CLETHROIDES	GOOSENECK PLANT
MALVA ALCEA "FASTIGIATA"	ROSE MALLOW
MERTENSIA VIRGINICA	VIRGINIA BLUEBELL
RUDBECKIA FULGIDA "GOLDSTURM"	BLACK-EYED SUSAN
STACHYS BYZANTINA‡	LAMB'S EARS
TRADESCANTIA X ANDERSONIA "BLUE STONE"	SPIDERWORT

* Listed as *Campanula persiciflora* "Blue"
** Listed as "Matricaria Ultra Double White"

† Listed as *Hosta undulata* "Variegata"
‡ Listed as *Stachys lanata*

NATIVE
GARDENS

R.R.1, BOX 494
GREENBACK, TENNESSEE
37742
(615) 856-3350

This is a small, relatively new nursery. The owners, Ed Clebsch and Meredith Bradford-Clebsch, are self-described "Plant Freaks." They are particularly concerned about the depletion of native flora by those collecting plants, and they grow all their native perennial offerings from seed they have personally obtained from their trips; they do not take plants from their native habitat. They replace (if available) or refund in full if plants do not arrive in good health; notification must be made. There is a minimum order requirement. Since they offer four different sizes of plants, they will substitute—when necessary and at no extra charge—with the next larger size or a comparable smaller size. For example, I recently ordered three plants in the $4.25 size and received as substitutes six in the $2.50 size. Had I realized how large the $2.50 size was, I would have probably ordered that size in the first place. If you want no substitutions whatsoever, you can indicate this on the form and receive a refund.

EASY CARE PERENNIAL OFFERINGS

BOTANICAL NAME	POPULAR NAME
ACHILLEA MILLEFOLIUM	YARROW
ALLIUM SCHOENOPRASUM	CHIVES
ASCLEPIAS TUBEROSA	BUTTERFLY WEED
COREOPSIS LANCEOLATA	COREOPSIS
DICENTRA EXIMIA	BLEEDING HEART
ECHINACEA PURPUREA	PURPLE CONEFLOWER
EUPATORIUM COELESTINUM	PERENNIAL AGERATUM
MONARDA DIDYMA	BEE BALM
OENOTHERA FRUTICOSA	SUNDROPS
PHYSOSTEGIA VIRGINIANA	OBEDIENT PLANT
STACHYS BYZANTINA*	LAMB'S EARS

* Listed as Lamb's Ears under "Herbs"

PICCADILLY
FARM

1971 WHIPPOORWILL
ROAD
BISHOP, GEORGIA 30621
(404) 769-6516

Piccadilly Farm specializes in growing perennial plants for southern gardens. Visitors are encouraged to see the display garden, which features over 150 kinds of hostas, numerous perennials, and many wildflowers. There is a minimum purchase amount and a flat handling and postage charge. You must indicate on the order form if you will accept substitutes. Their guarantee is limited to this statement: "We cannot replace plants lost to causes beyond our control, nor do we assume any warranty as to life after transplanting. Claims for any cause must be made within 5 days after receipt of shipment." Plants are not packed particularly well.

EASY CARE PERENNIAL OFFERINGS

BOTANICAL NAME	POPULAR NAME
ANEMONE VITIFOLIA "ROBUSTISSIMA"	ANEMONE
ASCLEPIAS TUBEROSA	BUTTERFLY WEED
DICENTRA EXIMIA	BLEEDING HEART
ECHINACEA PURPUREA	PURPLE CONEFLOWER
HEUCHERA SANGUINEA	CORAL BELLS
LILIUM TIGRINUM	TIGER LILY
LYSIMACHIA CLETHROIDES	GOOSENECK PLANT
OENOTHERA FRUTICOSA	SUNDROPS
PHLOX DIVARICATA	PHLOX
RUDBECKIA FULGIDA "GOLDSTURM"	BLACK-EYED SUSAN
STOKESIA LAEVIS	STOKESIA, CORNFLOWER

THE
PRIMROSE PATH

R.D. 2, BOX 110
SCOTTDALE,
PENNSYLVANIA 15683
(412) 887-6756

Charles and Martha Oliver, the owners of this nursery, offer many native American plants plus a broad selection of other perennials. They have also instituted their own breeding program and have created new varieties of phlox, lobelia, and primula. Visitors are welcomed to their nursery but are urged to call beforehand. There is no minimum purchase requirement and shipping charges, based on an order's total amount, are 10 percent to the east of the Rockies and 15 percent to the west. You must indicate whether you will accept substitutes, and are asked to give suggestions. The Olivers do not publish their refund policy; plants, however, are well packaged.

EASY CARE PERENNIAL OFFERINGS

BOTANICAL NAME	POPULAR NAME
ALLIUM SCHOENOPRASUM	CHIVES
AQUILEGIA VULGARIS	COLUMBINE
ASCLEPIAS TUBEROSA	BUTTERFLY WEED
BOLTONIA ASTEROIDES "SNOWBANK"	BOLTONIA
CAMPANULA PERSICIFOLIA	BELLFLOWER
COREOPSIS LANCEOLATA	COREOPSIS
DICENTRA EXIMIA	BLEEDING HEART
ECHINACEA PURPUREA	PURPLE CONEFLOWER
HEUCHERA SANGUINEA	CORAL BELLS
IBERIS SEMPERVIRENS	CANDYTUFT
MONARDA DIDYMA	BEE BALM
OENOTHERA FRUTICOSA	SUNDROPS
ONOCLEA SENSIBILIS	FERNS
PHLOX DIVARICATA	PHLOX
PLATYCODON GRANDIFLORUS	BALLOON FLOWER
POLEMONIUM REPTANS	JACOB'S LADDER
SEDUM SPECTABILE	SEDUM
STACHYS BYZANTINA*	LAMB'S EARS

* Listed as *Stachys olympica*

SUNLIGHT
GARDENS

RT. 1, BOX 600-A
ANDERSONVILLE,
TENNESSEE 37705
(615) 494-8237

Sunlight Gardens is a family nursery, owned and tended by a husband and wife team with a combined total of thirty years of academic and horticultural experience. Marty Zenni and Andrea Sessions specialize in the wildflowers, ferns, and perennials of eastern North America. All their plants are nursery grown from seed or propagated vegetatively; they do not sell plants collected in the wild. If customers are not completely satisfied with an order, they must file a claim for a refund or a replacement within thirty days. There is a minimum purchase requirement, but no shipping charges. You are asked to indicate on the order form what, if any, substitutions you are willing to accept.

EASY CARE PERENNIAL OFFERINGS

BOTANICAL NAME	PLANT NAME
ACHILLEA MILLEFOLIUM	YARROW
ASCLEPIAS TUBEROSA	BUTTERFLY WEED
BRUNNERA MACROPHYLLA	BUGLOSS
COREOPSIS LANCEOLATA	COREOPSIS
DICENTRA EXIMIA	BLEEDING HEART
ECHINACEA PURPUREA	PURPLE CONEFLOWER
EUPATORIUM COELESTINUM	PERENNIAL AGERATUM
MERTENSIA VIRGINICA	VIRGINIA BLUEBELL
MONARDA DIDYMA	BEE BALM
OENOTHERA FRUTICOSA	SUNDROPS
PHYSOSTEGIA VIRGINIANA	OBEDIENT PLANT
PLATYCODON GRANDIFLORUS	BALLOON FLOWER
POLEMONIUM REPTANS	JACOB'S LADDER
RUDBECKIA FULGIDA "GOLDSTURM"	BLACK-EYED SUSAN
STOKESIA LAEVIS	STOKESIA, CORNFLOWER

WAYSIDE
GARDENS
HODGES,
SOUTH CAROLINA
29695-0001
1-800-845-1124

The American Horticultural Society's 1988 Commercial Award was presented to Wayside Gardens, citing the firm's high standards and significant contributions to gardening. Wayside was started in 1920, and throughout the years has introduced many superb plants to American gardens. Their catalogue is filled with gorgeous pictures and enticing descriptions. Many of the offerings are difficult to grow, however, and are better suited to sophisticated gardeners. Beginners should probably start with the easy care plants described in this book. Probably because of the overall variety of offerings and the extensive care to ensure quality production, prices are quite high.

Wayside has a horticulturist to answer consumer questions on their toll-free number. There is no minimum purchase requirement. Shipping and handling charges are approximately 10 percent of an order sent east of the Mississippi and 15 percent for those west. Indicate on the order form whether you will accept substitutes. For spring shipments, you are given until September 1 to report failures and request refunds. I can personally testify that this is done in a prompt and courteous manner.

EASY CARE PERENNIAL OFFERINGS

BOTANICAL NAME	POPULAR NAME
ANEMONE VITIFOLIA "ROBUSTISSIMA"	ANEMONE
ARTEMISIA LUDOVICIANA VAR. ALBULA "SILVER KING"	SILVER KING
ASCLEPIAS TUBEROSA	BUTTERFLY WEED
ASTER X FRIKARTII "WONDER OF STAFFA"	ASTER FRIKARTII
ASTILBE X ARENDSII	ASTILBE
BOLTONIA ASTEROIDES "SNOWBANK"	BOLTONIA
BRUNNERA MACROPHYLLA	BUGLOSS
LILIUM TIGRINUM	TIGER LILY
LYTHRUM SALICARIA "MORDEN PINK"	LYTHRUM
MALVA ALCEA "FASTIGIATA"	ROSE MALLOW
MERTENSIA VIRGINICA	VIRGINIA BLUEBELL
POLEMONIUM REPTANS*	JACOB'S LADDER
RUDBECKIA FULGIDA "GOLDSTURM"**	BLACK-EYED SUSAN

* Plans to offer by 1990
** Offers both seed and vegetatively grown plants

WHITE
FLOWER FARM
LITCHFIELD, CONNECTICUT
06759-0050
(203) 496-9600 (orders)
(203) 496-1661
(customer service)

The White Flower Farm catalogue is called *The Garden Book* and costs $5. It's the most expensive nursery catalogue on the market and yet remains a bargain, filled with gorgeous colored photographs and some of the finest writing in the field (no pun intended). Plant prices are a bit high and the descriptions tend to be overly optimistic; nevertheless, the great variety of offerings is appreciated and the cultural information useful. In addition, a staff horticulturist is available weekdays to answer phone questions.

The store and gardens are a major tourist attraction in the Litchfield area.

With regard to refunds, the catalogue waffles a bit and states: "Refunds, where appropriate, are made promptly." There is no minimum purchase requirement but you must indicate on the order form your willingness to accept substitutes. Shipping charges are leveled on the total amount of the order and vary by location; generally, they are 10 percent for shipments east of the Mississippi and 15 percent for those west.

EASY CARE PERENNIAL OFFERINGS

BOTANICAL NAME	POPULAR NAME
ALLIUM SCHOENPRASUM	CHIVES
ASCLEPIAS TUBEROSA	BUTTERFLY WEED
ASTER X FRIKARTII "WONDER OF STAFFA"	ASTER FRIKARTII
ASTER NOVI-BELGII	NEW YORK ASTER
ASTILBE X ARENDSII	ASTILBE
BOLTONIA ASTEROIDES "SNOWBANK"	BOLTONIA
BRUNNERA MACROPHYLLA*	BUGLOSS
CAMPANULA PERSICIFOLIA**	BELLFLOWER
CENTAUREA MONTANA	MOUNTAIN BLUET

* Listed as *Anchusa myosotidiflora*
** Listed as *Campanula persicifolia "Telham Beauty"*